PUBLICATIONS PAQUETTE

www.paquettepublications.com

1st Edition

Complex Financial Power of Attorney

Legal Forms for Your Estate Planning Needs
with Supporting Documents

Paul M. Paquette

FIRST EDITION

© 2018, 2019						
Book Design:	Paul M. Paquette	**Proofread:**	Paul M. Paquette	**CD/USB:**	Paul M. Paquette
Front Cover:	Paul M. Paquette	**Editor:**	Paul M. Paquette	**Printing:**	N/A
Back Cover:	Paul M. Paquette	**Glossary:**	Paul M. Paquette	**Company:**	Paquette Publications
Cover Photo:	Zadorozhnyi Viktor	**Index:**	N/A	**Location:**	Auburn, KY - USA

Author: Paquette, Paul M.

Title: Complex Financial Power of Attorney

Subtitle: Legal Forms for Your Estate Planning Needs with Supporting Documents

Identifiers:	978-1-948389-02-0 PB	978-1-948389-16-7 HC	978-1-948389-19-8 SB/CB	978-1-948389-15-0 EBK: PDF
Classification:	LCCN: 2018900392	DDC: 346.7302/9—dc23		
Subject:	1. Law	2. Power of Attorney	3. Practical Guides	4. Estate Planning

PCIP:
Paquette, Paul., 1982 –
Complex Financial Power of Attorney:
Legal Forms for Your Estate Planning Needs with Supporting Documents (Estate Planning Series)
by Paul Paquette --1st ed.--Auburn, KY.: Paquette Publications. c2018, c2019 p. ; cm + CD-ROM (4.75")
ISBN - 13: 978-1-948389-02-0 (PB). -- ISBN - 13: 978-1-948389-16-7 (HC). --
ISBN - 13: 978-1-948389-19-8 (SB/CB). -- ISBN - 13: 978-1-948389-15-0 (EBK: PDF).
1. Power of attorney--United States--Popular works. 2. Power of attorney--United States--Forms.
3. Estate Planning--United States--Popular works. 4. Estate planning--United States--Forms. I. Title II. Series

Summary: The book consists of (**01**) one Complex Power of Attorney (Financial), (**16**) sixteen Supporting Documents, (**05**) five Miscellaneous Forms, (**03**) three Recommended Forms, and (**04**) four Appendix. This Power of Attorney has an estate planning focus that provides options, depth, and flexibility while maintaining uniformity with built-in and optional safety features.

Publication Media: Paquette Publications publishes in various formats (print, electronic, and print-on-demand). Some independent purchases or material included with the standard print versions may not be available in e-books or print-on-demand. If physical media (CD, DVD, or USB Drive) is not available within the book, then said files are downloadable online in digital format.

Digital Formats: Power of Attorney, Supporting Documents, Forms (Miscellaneous / Recommended), Worksheets, and Appendices are available in the following digital formats (PDF, DOCX, DOC, and ODT).

Bulk Purchases: Purchases of titles by Paquette Publications may occur in bulk for educational, business, fund-raising, or sale promotional use. For information, please email the following: **paquettepublications@gmail.com**.

Commercial License: Commercial Licensing is available upon request. Please direct all inquiries regarding the terms, conditions, and pricing to the following email: **paquettepublications@gmail.com**. In the email, please include the following: (**01**) Full Name and Title; (**02**) Name of Corporation and Address; (**03**) Corporate Status: Government, Non-Profit, or For-Profit; (**04**) Specific Intellectual Property in question; and (**05**) Purpose or intended use of Intellectual Property.

Questions: Please send all questions, suggestions, comments, and permission requests to the following email: **paquettepublications@gmail.com**.

Please Note: The purpose of this Publication(s) and its design is to provide accurate and authoritative information concerning the subject matter covered. The author has striven to use simple/plain English to clarify complex issues and make understanding/comprehension usable and intuitive. Due to the changing nature of law in the United States of America, the author makes the following **Legal Disclaimers & Waivers** on page iv.

Legal Disclaimers & Waivers

Definitions of Terms: The term "Publication(s)" shall refer, but are not limited, to the following: Power of Attorney, Supporting Documents, Worksheets, Miscellaneous Forms, Recommended Forms, and Appendices.

Waiver of Damages: The Purchaser or User of this Publication(s) agrees by default and understands the following: (**01**) The Organization, Distributor, Sales Representative, Publisher, or Author makes no guarantees of any kind or nature. (**02**) The Organization, Distributor, Sales Representative, Publisher, or Author assumes no liability for any or all damages resulting from utilizing this Publication(s) or reliance thereof. (**03**) Modification of this Publication(s) is permissible to suit a particular Purchaser or User need; however, the Purchaser or User assumes all risk.

No Representation of Services: The Purchaser or User of this Publication(s) agrees by default and understands the following: (**01**) The Organization, Distributor, Sales Representative, Publisher, or Author is not engaged in rendering professional services regarding medical, financial, legal, et cetera. (**02**) This Publication(s) is not a substitute for advice from a competent licensed professional.

Forum – Selection / Jurisdiction / Governing Law: The Purchaser or User of this Publication(s) agrees by default and understands the following: (**01**) The selection for governing law, venue, forum, and jurisdiction for all litigation shall exclusively be at the locality of the Organization (State of Incorporation) or the Author (State of Residence). (**02**) The Purchaser or User waives their right to choose, object, or make claims (economic hardship, unreasonable constraints, or inconvenience) concerning the governing law, venue, forum, and jurisdiction for all litigation against the Organization, Distributor, Sales Representative, Publisher, or Author. (**03**) Furthermore, the governing law, venue, forum, and jurisdiction may be further restricted based on City and County; please refer to "Additional Terms & Conditions" for more information.

Force / Mandatory Arbitration: The Purchaser or User of this Publication(s) agrees by default and understands the following: (**01**) All litigation, claims, disputes, settlements, judgments, lawsuits, or proceedings (governmental, administrative, governmental investigation, inquiries, hearing, request, or any appeal thereof) against the Organization, Distributor, Sales Representative, Publisher, or Author shall only go through force and binding arbitration with no other alternative legal recourse. (**02**) The arbitration shall be confidential in adherence to the Commercial Arbitration Rules of the American Arbitration Association. (**03**) Any judgment on the award rendered by the Arbitrator may be entered in any court having jurisdiction thereof or having jurisdiction over the relevant party or its assets. (**04**) The arbitration shall be performed by one (**01**) mutually agreed upon Arbitrator with experience in contract law. The arbitration shall be in English. (**05**) The Purchaser or User shall bear their costs in the arbitration with no right or award for reimbursement.

Injunctive Relief: The Purchaser or User agrees by default and understands that unauthorized access to or use of this Publication(s) that violates the limited or commercial license shall result in injunctive remedies (or an equivalent type of urgent legal relief) in any jurisdiction without providing notice or opportunity to cure.

Aggregate Liability: The Purchaser or User of this Publication(s) agrees by default and understands that the total aggregate liability arising out of or in connection with your use of or inability to use the Paquette Publications websites or Content contained thereon (whether in contract, tort, or otherwise) shall not exceed the monetary amount received by the Organization, Distributor, Sales Representative, Publisher, or Author from the Purchaser or User.

Class Action Waiver: The Purchaser or User of this Publication(s) agrees by default and understands the following: (**01**) To bring only claims in an individual capacity, not as a Class Member/Plaintiff/Petitioner in any class, consolidation, or proceeding (mass or representative). (**02**) The Arbitrator shall not consolidate more than one person's claim nor preside over any form of class, consolidation, or proceeding (mass or representative) unless the Defendant/Respondent agrees in writing to such actions in advance.

Additional Terms & Conditions: The Purchaser or User of this Publication(s) agrees by default and understands that their legal and consumer rights are restricted and legally bound to any/all updated Additional Terms & Conditions set forth on **www.paquettepublications.com** without prior or future notice. The Additional Terms & Conditions URL links are at the bottom of the home page: Legal Disclaimers & Waivers, License & Trademark, and All Rights Reserved.

Note of Caution: When filling out this Publication(s), please consider the following. The Purchaser or User should seek a legal professional's advice if the Purchaser or User is less than eighteen (18) years of age and currently deemed mentally incompetent or incapacitated. Feel free to utilize this Publication(s) as a template. However, without legal representation in the situation above, this Publication(s) would suffer litigation by Interested Third Parties and more than likely receive judgment as invalid. Remember, an active lawful court order covering the subject matter within this Publication(s) will always take precedence if a conflict occurs. **Please Note:** If the Purchaser or User does have an active court order. The Purchaser or User can design this Publication(s), so it is not in conflict; however, seek the advice of a legal professional if there are any questions.

Legal Questions: Practicing law without a license is a crime that comes with some hefty fines in the United States of America. To avoid the appearance of impropriety, the Author will not dispense any legal advice or provide any legal services. Furthermore, no Author of any self-help legal book will willfully give legal advice or services due to liability reasons. If the Purchaser or User has a legal question(s), seek out the advice of a competent licensed Attorney.

"What we do [in life], echoes in eternity."
~ Marcus Aurelius

Paul M. Paquette

Is a Western Kentucky University alumnus with a Financial Planning and Management degree.

He is a military veteran in the United States Army with eight years of experience as a Financial Management Technician.

Insurance & Securities License.

Free Thinker & Entrepreneur.

Favorite hobbies include coin collecting, watching movies, genealogy, camping, hiking, fishing, reading, and cooking.

PUBLICATIONS
AQUETTE

"An ounce of prevention is worth a pound of cure." ~ Benjamin Franklin

Overview & Perspective

Importance of Agent(s) Selection: In the Author's opinion, a Power of Attorney (POA) is the most powerful legal document a person can execute for estate planning purposes. Thus, the Principal should think long and hard when choosing an Agent. The Principal should seek a **Reliable**, **Trustworthy**, and **Competent** Agent(s). Do not shirk in doing one's due diligence regarding Agent selections; if doubts or concerns exist, suggest utilizing the various optional safety features available within the POA.

Categories of POA: The Author breaks down a POA into the following four categories: (**01**) Simple, (**02**) Complex, (**03**) Durable, and (**04**) Special. A **Simple POA** is for short-term (less than five years) use with an Agent whose honor is beyond reproach and doubt. A **Complex POA** is for long-term (greater than five years) use, preferably with multiple Agents to reflect the changing realities of life with optional safety features that create additional administrative burdens but with checks and balances on the Agent's power. A **Durable POA** is, in essence, a Complex POA; however, the durability provisions are already active. A **Special POA** is, in essence, a Simple POA best used spartanly with a limited scope and purpose.

Various Type of POA: Within the various categories of POA are the following types that the Author has written or plans to write so far:

- **Simple POA:** (**01**) Limited, (**02**) Banking, (**03**) Financial, (**04**) General, (**05**) Real Estate, and (**06**) Minor.
- **Complex POA:** (**01**) Limited, (**02**) Banking, (**03**) Financial, (**04**) General, (**05**) Real Estate, and (**06**) Minor.
- **Durable POA:** (**01**) Protecting, (**02**) Final Disposition, (**03**) Health Care, and (**04**) Health Care of Minor.
- **Special POA:** (**01**) Taxes, (**02**) Vehicles, and (**03**) Pets.

Principal: A Principal is a person who establishes a POA. The Principal names an Agent and bestows that person the ability to perform actions on the Principal's behalf.

Agent: An Agent serves in a fiduciary capacity on behalf of the Principal. This fiduciary position is usually voluntary. Monetary compensation and reimbursement usually occur if the Principal has the financial means. The POA outlines the Agent's powers along with any goals and objectives.

Delegate: A Delegate (non-acting Agent) serves on behalf of the acting Agent currently in power. This discretionary power is useful when the acting Agent suffers inconveniences due to a lack of knowledge, logistics issues, or time constraints. This optional safety feature is only available for Complex and Durable POAs.

Protector: A Protector safeguards the best interest/wishes of the Principal (primarily in a passive capacity) and provides basic administrative support (ensuring transparency) to the Agent. However, if the Agent violates their role as a Fiduciary, it is the role of the Protector to step in, relieve the Agent, and protect the Principal's rights and interests. To utilize a Protector, a Durable Protecting POA must proactively occur first to bestow such power to the Agent who shall serve as a Protector. This optional safety feature is only available for Complex and Durable POAs.

Supporting Documents: These supporting documents accompany the POA for administrative purposes; these documents are optional (may be required). The Agent's forms are as follows: (**01**) **Acknowledgment of Appoint by Agent**, (**02**) **Acknowledgment of Resignation by Agent**, (**03**) **Affidavit of Full Force and Effect**, (**04**) **Delegation of Agent's Power**, (**05**) **Revocation of Delegate by Agent**, and (**06**) **Co-Agent Agreement**. The Principal's forms are as follows: (**01**) **Revocation in Whole**, (**02**) **Revocation in Part(s)**, (**03**) **Revocation of Agent**, and (**04**) **Revocation of Delegate by Principal**. The Protector's forms are as follows: (**01**) **Acknowledgment of Appoint by Protector**, (**02**) **Acknowledgment of Resignation by Protector**, (**03**) **Revocation of Agent by Protector**, and (**04**) **Revocation of Delegate by Protector**. The Delegate's forms are as follows: (**01**) **Acknowledgment of Appoint by Delegate** and (**02**) **Acknowledgment of Resignation by Delegate.**

Forms Miscellaneous: These forms are available for the Principal; however, they are optional. Each document can stand alone and be extremely useful; think of it as an administrative support document that will make the Agent's life easier. These forms are as follows: (**01**) **Statement of Wishes**, (**02**) **Personal Information Worksheet**, (**03**) **Notification / Contact List**, (**04**) **Personal Documents Locator**, and (**05**) **Legal Document Locator**.

Forms Recommended: These forms are available for the Principal; however, they are optional. Each document can stand alone and be extremely useful; think of it as an administrative support document that will make the Agent's life easier. These forms are (**01**) **Affidavit of Principal's Health State** and (**02**) **Assets & Liabilities Worksheet**.

Appendices: These appendices are available for the Principal; however, these documents are optional (may be required). Each appendix can stand alone and be extremely useful; think of it as an administrative support document that will make the Agent's life easier. These appendices are as follows: (**01**) **Appendix A: Insurance Suggestions & Resource Guide**, (**02**) **Appendix B: Directions for Prudent & Safe Investing**, (**03**) **Appendix C: Attorney Suggestions & Resource Guide**, and (**04**) **Appendix D: Steps for Credit Repair & Statute of Limitations.**

"The evil that men do lives after them; the good is oft interred with their bones." ~ William Shakespeare

Be Pragmatic - Not Idealistic

The Principal should take great stride in being practical, especially regarding the nature of Power, Money, Time Management, and Motivation. Just because the Principal writes down what they want an Agent to do and bestows power to an Agent does not mean that the Principal's objectives will occur. For the Principal's objective to become a reality, there must be proper incentives or a great underlying sense of duty and honor. The Principal should read the topics below and evaluate their estate-planning situation realistically. Failure to do so otherwise will result in disaster.

Communication: Before drafting a Power of Attorney (**POA**), the Principal should take the time and make a phone call to the potential Agent(s) to verify if the Agent(s) are willing to act on the Principal behalf in a fiduciary manner. **Rhetorical Questions:** What is the point of appointing an Agent in a POA if the Agent declines to act later?

Administrative: When implementing a POA, make sure that all Agent(s) have an Original Notarized POA for their personal use in their possession. Failure to provide each Agent(s) with an Original Notarized POA will prevent or hinder their ability to execute the Principal's goals, objectives, and wishes. If the Agent(s) is completely unaware of the Principal's POA existence, do not expect anything to occur. A POA is useless if placed in a dresser drawer; remember to give the POA to the Agent(s).

Most businesses and institutions want to see the original notarized POA before letting the Agent(s) act for the Principal. The business or institution will usually make a copy of the original notarized POA for their file.

Transparency: Transparency begins with the Principal. If the Principal only provides POA to one of the Agents but not the others, it is foolhardy to expect an Agent to make copies and inform other Agent(s) and Third Parties of the Principal's POA.

Knowledge is power; an Agent will most likely not inform other legitimate Third Parties of the limits of their power. Thus, transparency is paramount to equalize the knowledge deficit that may exist and prevent such abuse of power.

Financial Resources: Do not expect an Agent(s) to perform out of the kindness of their heart and from their pockets. Be prepared to monetary reimburse the Agent(s) for their time and effort.

If the Principal wants specific actions to occur, ensure financial resources are available to achieve those objectives. Do not expect the Agent(s) to finance and pay for the Principal's objectives and wishes.

Write Clearly: When writing provisions and directives within the POA, the Principal must accomplish the following:
(01) The Principal must write clearly, as to what the Principal wants the Agent(s) to achieve;
(02) The Principal must not be vague, inconsistent, or conflicting about their intent and desires.

Co-Agents: **Current Situation:** When deciding to use Co-Agents (only available for Complex and Durable POA) as a form of checks and balances, the Principal would be wise to consider the following:

Questions to Ask: Do the Co-Agents have issues with one another? Have the Co-Agents ever worked together; if so, were there any issues or conflicts? Are there known social issues or grievances between the Co-Agents? Are the relationship dynamics between the Co-Agents confrontational, thus hindering the Principal's POA objectives?

Rhetorical Questions: What is the point of having Co-Agents, especially if both Agents have issues working together?

Pragmatic Reality: If Co-Agents cannot work together, instead of protecting the Principal's interests, the Co-Agents are more likely to prevent actions from occurring, thus delaying the Principal's wishes. When time is of the essence - this is usually detrimental.

Delegate: **Current Situation:** When deciding to use Delegate (only available for Complex and Durable POA), the Principal would be wise to consider the following:

Questions to Ask: Does the Principal have property or assets in more than one physical location? Do certain Agents have specific skill sets that other Agents do not process?

Rhetorical Questions: If an Agent defers some of their responsibility to a Delegate, will the Principal have issues with that?

Pragmatic Reality: Consider using a Delegate if the Principal current situation is complex. The more flexibility the Agent(s) has in implementing the Principal's objectives. The more likely, those objectives will become a reality.

Protector: **Current Situation:** When deciding to use Protector (only available for Complex and Durable POA) as a form of checks and balances, the Principal would be wise to consider the following:

Questions to Ask: Does the Principal have trust issues with any of the Agent(s) selected for the POA? Does the Principal believe that a Protector has enough willpower and devotion to keep the Agent(s) in check from exceeding their power and authority? Will the Protector be a pawn or bend to an Agent's will?

Rhetorical Questions: What is the point of having a Protector if the Protector decides not to enforce the terms and conditions of the POA to the best of their ability? Will the Protector be impartial and independent when using their powers?

Pragmatic Reality: If the Principal is considering a Protector to police the Agent's actions regarding the POA, then the Agent(s) for consideration are slim pickings. It will be highly advantageous to reconsider the Agent(s) selection. Consider only having one (**01**) Protector in charge that can make unilateral decisions versus hamstringing the Agent with Co-Agency. Most importantly, ensure the Principal selects the right Agent to serve as the Protector.

PUBLICATIONS

A
Q
U
E
T
T
E

"The best way to find yourself is to lose yourself in the service of others." ~ Mahatma Gandhi

To Dr. Edward Wolfe (Professor of Finance)

Thank you for the inspiration and educational opportunities.

Table of Contents

CHAPTER 01

CHAPTER

01

Introductions

CHAPTER 01

Overview

CHAPTER

01

Introductions

Overview

Chapter 01 provides the opportunity for the Author to communicate directly with the Reader (Purchaser or User) regarding the purpose and goals of this book. Furthermore, the Author briefly comments on the positive and negative attributes that the Reader (Purchaser or User) may encounter when using a self-help law book (Growing Trends, Cost/Value Analysis, Local Rules, Law Dynamics, and Legal Research).

- **Purpose of this Book** **(0.4 Pages Total)**
  Self-explanatory - outlines the author's primary motivation and answers the "why" question.

- **Goal of this Book** **(0.2 Pages Total)**
  Self-explanatory - outlines the author's goal and states what the author is trying to achieve.

- **Using Self – Help Law Books** **(0.1 Pages Total)**
  Highlights the advantages and disadvantages of doing one's legal work and expands on the topic below to include the following: Growing Trend, Cost / Value Analysis, Local Rules, and Changes in the Law.

- **Growing Trends** **(0.3 Pages Total)**
  The author's commentary explains why doing one's legal work has become a growing trend in today's society.

- **Cost / Value Analysis** **(0.4 Pages Total)**
  The author's commentary explains the economic benefits and value of doing one's legal work.

- **Local Rules** **(0.2 Pages Total)**
  The author's commentary explains how local rules can potentially affect a legal document's execution and legitimacy.

- **Law Dynamics** **(0.2 Pages Total)**
  The author's commentary explains how laws serve society and how the evolution of laws reflects society's needs.

- **Legal Research** **(0.2 Pages Total)**
  The author's commentary explains how to perform and research legal issues using various methodologies.

Purpose of this Book

In the Author's humble opinion and experience, most people need "living" legal documents that can adjust and "provide for breathing room" over time, with practical concepts and applications relevant to everyday life.

Through research and experience, the Author has analyzed numerous legal forms, with the majority sharing the following characteristics: (**01**) lack of detail and depth, (**02**) lack of options, and (**03**) very narrow in purpose or scope, especially when the subject matter is broad and vast. These deficiencies are primarily due to legal forms being locality or state-specific, usually deriving from the statutory form that had to meet the approval of some committee in which agendas (political, religious, and lobbyist) dictate available options. These statutory forms typically give a courteous overview of the subject matter in question without addressing the finer details and permeable conditions that one usually encounters in life. The lack of personal rights and liberties offer in statutory forms leaves little in the way of protection.

When Attorneys draft legal forms, these forms are usually premade with boilerplate language. Unless the client explicitly asks the Attorney to include specifics to address the eventualities that may occur with protective language in a disaster, said safety features are invisible. The lack of protectionism and detail is primarily due to the Attorney's inherent conflict of getting the job done in the least amount of time possible to maximize profits. Conversely, a client is usually unwilling to pay a high legal fee to compensate the Attorney for the time necessary to make said legal document "Iron Clad." A financial equilibrium develops when drafting a legal document with the unspoken agreement of "hey, this may not work in all life situations." Thus, the client may have to consult with an Attorney yet again and spend more money if an unanticipated situation occurs.

Power of Attorney is the focus of this book; within this book is (**01**) one Complex Power of Attorney (**Financial**), (**16**) sixteen Supporting Documents, (**05**) five Miscellaneous Forms, (**03**) three Recommended Forms, and (**04**) four Appendix. This Power of Attorney has an estate planning focus that provides options, depth, and flexibility while maintaining uniformity with built-in and optional safety features.

The Goal of this Book

The goal of the Author through this book is to provide legal forms with an estate planning focus that has options and depth while maintaining uniformity, thus offering clear directives that are flexible with built-in safety features that are inherently lacking in most legal forms.

The design of these legal forms within this book is for use in the United States of America. Use these legal forms as a template and adjust them appropriately with the help of a competent, licensed Attorney if the Purchaser or User lives in another country. These legal forms may be most applicable and adaptable to countries with a legal basis derived from Great Britain's common law approach; thus, any of Great Britain's current and former colonies are good candidates. Remember, laws from various countries differ; however, laws tend to converge to form some universal doctrine; this phenomenon has increased rapidly due to technological advancement, thus allowing for the greater exchange of ideas. **Please Note:** Not all countries are at the same convergence rate; countries with similar roots and thoughts will be closer to convergence. The disparity can be significant, especially regarding laws from two distinct and separate cultures.

The Author hopes that the goals stated in this book succeed or surpass the Purchaser's or User's expectations and give the Purchaser or User a sense of peace and security in their everyday life.

Using Self-Help Law Books

One should be aware of the inherent advantages and disadvantages of doing one's legal work. Thus, it behooves the Purchaser or User to understand the challenges and difficulties this may encompass. The Author will briefly discuss the following: Growing Trends, Cost/Value Analysis, Local Rules, Law Dynamics, and Legal Research when using self-help law books.

• Growing Trends

There has been a noticeable trend for Purchasers or Users to prepare their legal documents and handle their legal affairs versus hiring an Attorney. Courts across this country recognize that legal services are expensive and make every effort to make it easier for the individual(s) to represent themselves. However, on the reverse side of the coin, do not expect the courts to accommodate and provide sympathy for Purchaser or User who chooses not to utilize an Attorney. Some legal professionals and courts take the attitude, "want to save a buck, fine; however, if the Purchaser or User has any questions, go to the law library and figure it out."

The Author believes the Purchaser or User should have options, to make their lives easier and less confusing from a legal perspective. The Author tries to make these forms modular, universal, and easy to understand, with built-in directions. However, the Author cannot cover every conceivable possibility and include all the nuances due to local laws, statutes, and ruling. Thus, it is highly advantageous that the Purchaser or User seeks the advice of a competent, licensed State Attorney if clarification or additional help regarding legal issues is required.

• Cost / Value Analysis

The global marketplace offers many options when shopping for a product or service with various quality levels and price points. When deciding on purchasing a product or service, the Purchaser or User will internally make a cost/value analysis base on their willingness to pay for the desired quality.

Most legal situations are straightforward and require a simple form, no complex analysis, some intelligence, and the ability to follow instructions. In situations like these, it makes sense to do one's legal work to save money at the expense of a small amount of the Purchaser's or User's time. However, in special or unique situations that are incredibly complex, a personal approach is prudent; seek a licensed attorney who can provide such service. Do not be cheap, realize one's limitations, and admit when help is required.

Creating a self-help law book involving legal matters entails simplifying the laws and condensing several legal cases into a single sentence or paragraph. Due to such simplifications, complications may arise that only an Attorney will notice. Remember, this is not a law book; if it were, it would be about a thousand pages long and too complex for most people to understand. The simplification process does entail leaving out many details and nuances that may apply to unique or unusual situations. Depending on whose opinion and specialty, there may be several valid interpretations for a legal principle or basis; thus, the possibility exists that a Judge may disagree with the Author's analysis.

Therefore, when deciding to utilize a self-help law book and do one own legal work, a cost/value analysis occurs. The Purchaser or User has to decide to save money (money spent on an Attorney instead) by doing the legal work themself, thus calculating that their efforts will outweigh the chances of rejection for their case (legal matters). Most individuals deciding to handle their legal affairs never encounter a legal problem, but occasionally people find that it costs more to have an Attorney fix their problem than to hire an Attorney to deal with it in the beginning. The Author is not trying to dissuade the Purchaser or User from legal empowerment but only to disclose the risk when handling one's legal matters. Consult with a competent, licensed State Attorney if the Purchaser or User has any questions or needs guidance.

• Local Rules

This book is not all-inclusive; there are limitations regarding what a self-help law book can do for the Purchaser or User. One should be aware that there are bound to be procedural differences that vary from state to state, county to county, and potentially even Judge to Judge. The Purchaser or User should not expect to be able to get all the information and resources solely from within the confines of this book or any book. However, this book will serve as a guide to give the Purchaser or User-specific information whenever possible to help find out what else the Purchaser or User may need to know.

It is highly advantageous that before using any of the forms within this book, the Purchaser or User consults with their court clerk. The court clerks will inform the Purchaser or User if there are any local rules or forms that one should be aware of that are required. Usually, these forms will require the same information as the forms within this book but merely format differently, with slightly different wording, or using different color paper so that the clerk can quickly locate the document. The court clerk may ask for additional information to process the legal document.

• Law Dynamics

The law is not static and constant; it is ever-evolving and dynamic. Given enough time, social and political pressures will change the laws, thus reflecting the very fabric of our civilization, as age-old rulings are overturned and lie fallow. This book is not a reflection pool, nor is the Author a seer who can peer into the future. It behooves the Purchaser or User of this book to check for the most recent statutes, rules, and regulations to see if any changes have occurred since its publication.

In most cases, the changes in the law will be insignificant, for example, a redesigned form, extra information, or alteration to a waiting period. Thus, the Purchaser or User might need to revise a form, file another form, or wait for an additional time; these changes will not usually affect the outcome of a case / legal matter. However, significant changes occasionally happen, and the entire law in a particular area requires a new interpretation. A legal case that serves as the basis for a central legal point becomes invalid, null, or void, thus impairing the Purchaser's or User's legal goal. If there are unique local requirements or recent changes in the law, seek the advice of a competent, licensed Attorney.

• Legal Research

If the Purchaser or User needs additional information, consult the local law library, usually found at the county courthouse or a law school. Ask the librarian for assistance concerning the subject matter of interest. The primary source of information will be in the State's Statutes or Codes, with titles such as "Revised" or "Annotated" the title may include the publisher's name, and there could be more than one publisher. Ensure the Purchaser or User has the current version of their State laws. The most common way to update law books is a soft-cover supplement found on the back of each volume; other methods include supplement volume, loose-leaf bindings, and supplement sections. An additional source of legal information is as follows: Internet Research (suggests visiting **www.findlaw.com**); Practice manuals; Digest (gives summaries of appeals court cases); Case Reporter (contains full written opinions of appeals court cases); and Legal Encyclopedia (Major sets include ***American Jurisprudence*** and ***Corpus Juris Secundum***).

CHAPTER 02

CHAPTER

02

Instructions

CHAPTER 02

Overview

CHAPTER

02

Instructions

Overview

The following are stand-alone instructional pages for convenience purposes only; each document within this chapter comes with built-in instructions for easy completion. These stand-alone instructional pages may help clarify questions or provide additional insights that the Reader (Purchaser or User) may have.

- **POA's Legal Requirement** **(01 Pages Total)**
  The author explains the legal requirements, justifications, and prudent measures for the Principal, Witnesses, and Notary within the United States of America.

- **Instructions for Principal** **(01 Pages Total)**
  This (stand-alone) instructional page guides the Principal as to what their requirements are when it comes to filling out a Power of Attorney (Simple, Complex, Durable, and Special) within this book.

- **Instructions for Witnesses** **(01 Pages Total)**
  This (stand-alone) instructional page guides the Witnesses as to what their requirements are when it comes to filling out a Power of Attorney (Simple, Complex, Durable, and Special) within this book.

- **Instructions for Notary Public** **(01 Pages Total)**
  This (stand-alone) instructional page guides the Notary Public as to what their requirements are when it comes to filling out a Power of Attorney (Simple, Complex, Durable, and Special) and Supporting Documents within this book.

- **Built-In Safety Features** **(06 Pages Total)**
  These (stand-alone) instructional pages highlight the Built-in Safety Feature found in the Power of Attorney (Simple, Complex, Durable, and Special) within this book.

- **Optional Safety Features** **(06 Pages Total)**
  These (stand-alone) instructional pages highlight the Optional Safety Feature found predominately in this book's Power of Attorney (Complex and Durable).

POA's Legal Requirements

Not A Court Order:

A Power of Attorney (**POA**) is not a court order; the execution of this POA is strictly voluntary; implementation of the POA **must be proactive to be effective and valid**. Falsification of this POA may constitute a criminal offense.

Recordation:

It is highly advantageous (more acceptable to bank officials or other financial institutions) that the Principal record/file (usually optional) the POA with the courts/official state record keeper, usually at the county level known as "county recorder of deeds." Utilizing a POA for Real Estate Transactions will require recordation and a Thumb/Finger Print in the Execution and Signature Page. It is advisable to consult with a licensed Attorney or the County Recorder of Deeds if there are any special filing/recording requirements.

Various State Laws:

As of 2011, every State within the U.S.A. has enacted the Uniform Power of Attorney Act (UPOAA) except for Louisiana; however, each State may have differences concerning the legal requirements relating to the execution of a POA. All States require that the Principal (the person enacting the POA) sign and date the POA. Depending upon the State, the requirements for Witnesses are the following: (**01**) one or more Witnesses, (**02**) two Witnesses and a Notary Public, or (**03**) either two Witnesses or a Notary Public. In States where both a Witnesses and a Notary Public are requirements, some States require notarization of only the Principal's signature. In contrast, other states require notarization of the Principal and both Witnesses. Free notary services are usually within a Government Facility, Post Office, or Public Libraries.

Legal Prudence:

Due to the various legal requirements of each State, the POA within this book conforms to the most prudent of measures concerning Principal, Witnesses, and Notary Public requirements. Thus, every POA within this book requires the Principal Signature and Date, (**02**) two Witnesses Signature and Date, and a Notary Public attestation to the Principal and Witnesses Signature and Date, along with the Notary Public's Seal, Signature, and Date. By notarizing the POA, the Principal has made it extremely difficult for a Third Party to challenge the validity of the Principal's signature and intentions.

Principal Requirements:

Although not all states require the following concerning the Principal, it is a prudent practice that the Principal meets the following criteria to execute a POA (to prevent future legal challenges). (**01**) The Principal is at least eighteen (**18**) years or older. (**02**) The Principal is of sound and disposing mind (emotionally and mentally competent). (**03**) The Principal has the capacity with full memory or necessary mental faculties. (**04**) The Principal willfully and voluntarily executes this POA. **Please Note:** If the Principal is old and may exhibit signs of functioning non-socially, incapacitated, or incompetent in the future, it is highly advantageous that the Principal proactively implements an **Affidavit of Principal's Health State** before implementing a POA.

Witnesses and Notary Public Requirements:

Although not all states require the following concerning the Witnesses and Notary Public, it is a prudent practice that the Witnesses and Notary Public do not have a conflict of interest and thus be impartial during the execution process of the POA (this is to prevent future legal challenges). These criteria will be grounds for a conflict of interest if the Witnesses or Notary Public is one or more: (**01**) Any individual related to the Principal by blood, marriage, or adoption. (**02**) Any individual who is currently a Beneficiary of the Principal's estate (laws of intestate succession or any existing will/codicil). (**03**) Any individual who benefits from a financial policy (insurance or annuity), in which the Principal's life is the insured. (**04**) Any individual claiming (present/inchoate) any portion of the Principal's estate. (**05**) Any individual who serves as an Owner, Operator, or employee of a Health Care Facility (Medical, Mental, Assisted Living), in which the Principal is currently a Patient / Client unless the employee serves solely as a Notary Public. (**06**) Any Doctor, Physician, Psychologist, Psychiatrist, Social Worker, Financial Advisor, and Financial Manager in which the Principal is currently a Patient / Client. (**07**) Any individual who serves as an Owner, Operator, or employee of a Final Dispositional Facility (Funerary Home, Crematory Authority, and Cemetery Authority) unless the employee serves solely as a Notary Public. (**08**) Any individual who is an Agent (active/inactive) serving in a fiduciary capacity under this POA. (**09**) Upon the Principal death, any individuals or entities may have a claim (the creditor) against the Principal's estate. (**10**) Any individual under the age of eighteen (**18**) years or is currently incapacitated or incompetent. The Witnesses should be twenty-one (**21**) years of age or older.

Benefits:

The above requirements may seem burdensome and overzealous on the Author's part to impose upon the Principal, especially if the State of residency does not require all of these extra precautions; however, the end benefits are well worth it. By enacting these prudent measures concerning the Principal, Witnesses, and Notary --- companies, third-party service providers, and professionals (Doctors, Attorneys, Financial Advisers, et cetera) are more likely to honor the POA without questions. If the invocation of the POA was to occur in another State, the Principal could rest peacefully knowing that their POA would be just as effective and legitimate in that State.

Revocation:

When revoking a POA, two (**02**) Witnesses and a Notary Public are preferred; however, a Notary Public is a bare minimum requirement. Furthermore, a current **Affidavit of Principal's Health State** accompanying the Revocation is highly advantageous, especially if legally challenged in the future. All Revocation documents within this book require notarization.

Instructions

Instructions for Principal

A Principal is a person who implements (fills out and executes) a legal document (Power of Attorney) that gives power to another person named the Agent to interact with and create a legal arrangement with a Third Party.

Fill out the Identifying Information of the Key Individual (Principal, Agent, Protector):

Key Individual →

Full Name:

Address:

Phone #: **Email:**

Residence: **County:** **State:**

The following are selection choices in various formats that the Principal will encounter throughout the Power of Attorney.

"Y" or "N" Here ↑ Initial Here ↑

Place "Y" for Yes or "N" for No in the box and initial "✎" the line if the Principal desires the following:

(A) Effective Immediately

Place a "✓" in the box if the Principal desires the following:

Report Period: ☐ None ☐ Monthly ☐ Quarterly ☐ Annually

The Principal wants to establish an expiration date for this POA as stated below:

The date that POA Expires: Month of: ______ Day of: ______ Year of: ________

Fill out the Identifying Information of the Principal as shown in Signature and Execution:

Principal →

Full Legal Name:

Today's Date:

Signature: ✎

Thumb/Finger Print:

Real Estate Transaction

Optional Safety Feature: At the bottom of **each** page of the Legal document is a security device reference as the Security Footer; if the **Security Footer** setting is to "**Low**," "**Moderate**," or "**High**," then the **Principal** needs to initial the bottom of each page as designated below for that page to be valid and enforceable.

1st Witness: ______ **2nd Witness:** ______ **Notary Public:**______ **Principal:** ↙ ______

Instructions for Witnesses

A Witness(es) is a person(s) who signs their name to the legal documents for attestation purposes concerning the authenticity that the Principal has authorized a course of action.

The role of the Witness is to verify that the Principle is 18 years of age or older, has created said legal document, and did so of their free choice while in a state of mental and emotional competency. When selecting a witness, the criteria are as follows: 18 years or older (prefer 21 years), cannot benefit directly or indirectly from the Principal, unbiased party, and no immediate relation to the Principal. On the **Signature and Execution Page** is the following regarding the (02) two Qualified Adult Witnesses.

Have (02) two Adult Witness* the Principal's signature in addition to having their signature notarized*

In the joint presence of each other, the Witnesses State that the Principal is the following: (**01**) The Principal is at least eighteen (**18**) years or older. (**02**) The Principal is of sound and disposing mind (emotionally and mentally competent). (**03**) The Principal is not suffering from constraint, duress, fraud, or undue influence. (**04**) The Principal acknowledges having willfully and voluntarily dated and signed this POA (or asked/directed for such actions to occur). (**05**) The Witnesses affirm that they have no direct biological or marital relationship with the Principal and are not a Beneficiary of the Principal's estate. (**06**) The Witnesses affirm their impartiality and confirm that the criterion stated in the box at the bottom of the last page does not apply. (**07**) The Witnesses declare this paragraph true and correct under the Penalty of Perjury.

If the Witness is uncomfortable giving out personal contact information, current employment information and occupation will suffice.

1st Witness →	**Name:**		Signature:
	Address:		
	Phone #:		**Date:**
	Occupation:		

2nd Witness Or Special Witness ** →	**Name:**		Signature:
	Address:		
	Phone #:		**Date:**
	Occupation:		

Optional Safety Feature: At the bottom of **each** page of the Legal document is a security device reference as the Security Footer; if the **Security Footer** setting is "**High**," then the two (**02**) **Witness** need to initial the bottom of each page as designated below for that page to be valid and enforceable.

1st Witness: ______ **2nd Witness:** ______ **Notary Public:** ______ **Principal:** ______

Instructions for Notary Public

A Notary Public is a public officer constituted by law to serve the public in non-contentious matters. Whose primary functions are to **(01)** administer oaths/affirmations and **(02)** witness and authenticate the executions of the legal documents.

The Notary Public's role is to verify that the Principle is 18 years of age or older, has created said legal document, and did so of their free choice while in a state of mental and emotional competency. Furthermore, the Notary Public shall attest that witnesses have signed this document in their presence. When selecting a Notary Public, the criteria are as follows: 18 years or older (prefer 21 years), cannot benefit directly or indirectly from the Principal, unbiased party, and no immediate relation to the Principal. On the **Signature and Execution Page** is the following that relates to the Notary Public.

UNDER THE LAWS OF ➔ COUNTY: ____________________

STATE: ____________________

Before the Notary Public (the undersigned authority) comes forth, the Principal, with a sound/disposed mind, is eighteen (**18**) years or older. The Principal acknowledges having willfully and voluntarily dated and signed this POA (or asked/directed for such actions to occur) stated above in the Notary Public presence. If Witnesses sign and attest that the Principal has signed this POA, the Notary Public shall attest that the Witnesses have signed this POA in the Notary Public's presence. Furthermore, the Notary Public states that the Principal has provided a Government Issue identification card with a facial picture to prove identity. The Notary Public declares under the Penalty of Perjury that this paragraph is true and correct.

If the Principal or Witnesses sign this POA but not in the presence of the Notary Public, then the Notary Public will not notarize or sign this POA.

* Notary Public →			
	Full Name:		**Signature & Seal:**
	Location:		
	Address:		
	Phone #:		**I.D. Number:**
	Date:		**Commission Expires:**

Optional Safety Feature: At the bottom of **each** page of the Legal document is a security device reference as the Security Footer; if the **Security Footer** setting is **Moderate**" or "**High**," then the **Notary Public** needs to initial the bottom of each page as designated below for that page to be valid and enforceable.

1st Witness: ______ **2nd Witness:** ______ **Notary Public:** ______ **Principal:** ______

Built-In Safety Features

Built-in Safety Features

These documents come with **Built-in Safety Features** to protect the Principal; the following examples illustrate these safety features and explain why they exist.

Choice Selection: It allows the Principal to select "**Yes**" or "**No**" with either a **Y** or **N**; along with initialization, this allows for modulation and verification for choice selection.

Article III: Effective Date of POA

The Principal wants the following regarding the effective date for the legal enforcement of this POA: The Principal can choose from (**02**) two options; however, **options A** and **B** are mutually exclusive. **Option A** shall be the default option in the event of ambiguities.

Place "Y" for Yes or "N" for No in the box and initial "✐" the line if the Principal desires the following: **(A) Effective Immediately**

"Y" or "N" Here ↑ Initial Here ↑

By designating "Y" for Yes, the effective date of this POA shall begin from the day of execution, as stated in **Article XXI**. If durability provision(s) are active in **Article XIV**, those provision(s) shall immediately take effect.

Place "Y" for Yes or "N" for No in the box and initial "✐" the line if the Principal desires the following: **(B) Effective if Events are Trigger**

"Y" or "N" Here ↑ Initial Here ↑

By designating "Y" for Yes, the effective date of this POA shall begin when such events transpire or occur, as outlined in **Article V**: "**Springing Powers**." If durability provision(s) are active in **Article XIV**, the durability provision(s) shall be active when such events transpire, as outlined in **Article V**: "**Springing Powers**."

Agent Conflict of Interest: This Safety feature protects the Principal from conflict of interest and situations where the Principal's financial interest may be at stake.

Article VII: Designation of Agent

The Principal should only designate an Agent if that individual is **Reliable**, **Trustworthy**, and **Competent** to manage the Principal's affairs. For legal reasons, all Agents must be competent and at least eighteen (**18**) years or older. None of the following individuals (non-relative) may serve as the Principal's Agent. (**A**) Any individual who serves as an Owner, Operator, or employee of a Health Care Facility (Medical, Mental, or Assisted Living) in which the Principal is currently a Patient / Client unless the employee serves solely as a Notary Public. (**B**) Any individual who serves as an Owner, Operator, or employee of a Final Dispositional Facility (Funerary Home, Crematory Authority, and Cemetery Authority) unless the employee serves solely as a Notary Public. (**C**) Any Doctor, Physician, Psychologist, Psychiatrist, Social Worker, Financial Advisor, or Financial Manager in which the Principal is currently a Patient / Client. Automatic Revocation of the Spouse designation as Agent shall occur if the following happens: (**01**) Dissolution or annulment of the marriage. (**02**) Proceedings are currently active for Dissolution of Marriage. (**03**) The Principal currently lives in a separate physical location from their Spouse for more than (**02**) two months with the intention of a divorce. The Principal designates the following individual as the Agent, the first choice, with decision-making powers in adherence to the terms and conditions specified in this POA.

Built-in Safety Features

These documents come with **Built-in Safety Features** to protect the Principal; the following examples illustrate these safety features and explain why they exist.

Yellow Space: This Safety feature ensures that the Principal can write in additional directions or terms (conditions, prohibitions, restrictions, exceptions, additions, limitations, extensions, and special rules). Option One (**01**) requires the writing to be " **Type.**" Option Two (**02**) requires the writing to be "**Type**" or "**Legible writing in Ink**" but not both.

Option One (01):		
Specify in Detail		Must be Type

Option Two (02):		
Specify in Detail		Preferably Type or Legible writing in Ink

Restrictions on Agent's Power: This Safety feature protects the Principal from actions that the Agent may do that are harmful to the Principal.

Article X: Restrictions on Agent's Powers

A: Regardless of what authorization or powers bestow in **Article VII_Subsection A through X,** the Agent shall not do or perform the following: **(01)** The Agent shall not make a loan to oneself, another name Agent, or a beneficiary of the Agent. **(02)** The Agent shall not take a service fee as an Agent. **(03)** The Agent shall not create, modify, or revoke a trust. **(04)** The Agent shall not use the Principal's property to fund a trust for someone other than the Principal or a trust that does not benefit the Principal greater than seventy (70%) percent. **(05)** The Agent shall not create or change a Beneficiary's interest in the Principal's property. **(06)** The Agent shall not create or change the Principal's interest in the Principal's property solely for the benefit of another. **(07)** The Agent shall not designate or change the designation of beneficiaries to receive any property, benefit, or contract right on the Principal's death. **(08)** The Agent shall not make or revoke a gift of the Principal property in trust or another arrangement. **(09)** The Agent shall not make or revoke a gift on the Principal behalf. **(10)** The Agent shall not exercise any powers that would cause the Principal's assets to become taxable to the Agent or the Agent's estate for any income, estate, or inheritance tax. **(11)** The Agent shall not forgive debts owed to the Principal, disclaim, or waive benefits payable to the Principal. **(12)** The Agent shall not execute, publish, declare, amend, or revoke the following: last will, codicil, or any will substitute on the Principal's behalf. **(13)** The Agent shall not perform duties under a contract that requires the Principal's services. **(14)** The Agent shall not make an affidavit about the Principal's knowledge that is unknown to the Agent personally. **(15)** The Agent shall not vote in any governmental public election on behalf of the Principal unless the Agent has a notarized letter stating who the Principal's candidates and voting preferences are regarding that public election. **(16)** The Agent shall not exercise powers and authority granted to the Principal as Trustee or a court-appointed Fiduciary. **(17)** The Agent shall not exercise the right to make a disclaimer on behalf of the Principal, except for a disclaimer of a detrimental transfer or acceptance made with the court's approval. **(18)** The Agent shall not enjoin (add or transfer) ownership or title to the Principal's funds or assets in the Agent's name alone. **Please Note:** Waiver of these restrictions shall only occur if the Principal grants written permission in **Article IX Subsection Y**.

Built-in Safety Features

These documents come with **Built-in Safety Features** to protect the Principal; the following examples illustrate these safety features and explain why they exist.

Additional Legal Provisions: These safety features protect the Principal.

Modifications: Ensure the document's legitimacy and integrity.

N: Modification: Changes or modifications to this POA shall not occur upon execution. If the Principal wants to change this POA, the Principal must make an entirely new one. However, revocation of any part(s) of this POA may occur if it is in writing; once a part(s) receives revocation, it shall be permanent. Alterations (strikes out, cross out, and blackouts) of any provisions or writing within this POA shall have no bearing in a court of law and shall remain active and valid as to their original intent.

Picture I.D.: Ensure the legitimacy of the Agent.

O: Picture I.D.: The Principal requires verifying the Agent's identity with a government-issued picture ID. The Principal does not require it to be current and up to date; all that the Principal requires is the ability to confirm their facial features in a picture from an official governmental source.

Governing Law: Determines which laws and jurisdiction shall take priority if a legal issue arises.

T: Governing Law: This POA shall take effect immediately as a sealed instrument and shall receive interpretation, enforcement, and governance under the State's laws where the Principal has established physical residency at the time of enforcement. The Principal requests for the honoring of this POA in any State, County, or Location in which the Principal's body or property may be, with the intention that it be valid in all jurisdictions/territories of the United States and all Foreign Nations. This POA is to receive the most liberal interpretation available to grant the appointed Fiduciary the greatest amount of decision-making discretion.

Severability / Saving Clause: This clause ensures the survival and permanency of the legal document if certain sections or provisions are illegal or invalid.

U: Severability / Saving Clause: An invalid or unenforceable provision within this POA might exist. If that occurs, the remaining provisions of this POA shall continue and be active as if said invalid or unenforceable provision did not exist. All remaining provisions shall be undisturbed to maintain their original legal meaning, force, and effect. If a court finds or deems that an invalidated or unenforceable provision will become valid if limitations exist, then such written provision shall receive a written modification by court order to limit the provision's power while maximizing the economic value and liberties granted.

Court Appointed of Guardian or Conservator: The Principal can nominate an individual in advance if the Courts decide upon a Guardian or Conservator.

X: Court Appointed Guardian or Conservator: the Principal intends by this POA to avoid a court-supervised guardianship or conservatorship. If the Principal attempts or fails to avoid a court-supervised guardianship or conservatorship. Then, the Principal requests that the Agent designated in this POA serve as Guardian or Conservator of the Principal's property and affairs. The court-appointed Guardian or Conservator shall not have the power to revoke, suspend, or terminate this POA or the Agent's powers except as specifically authorized by law. The Principal may execute the following: "**Declaration in Advance of Need for Guardianship & Conservatorship**," if execution occurs, the Principal prefers that those individuals act in such a fiduciary capacity.

Built-in Safety Features

These documents come with **Built-in Safety Features** to protect the Principal; the following examples illustrate these safety features and explain why they exist.

Acknowledgment by the Agent: A basic overview of the Agent's Responsibility; this is to prevent the Agent from using the excuse "I did not know" and so forth. Furthermore, since this Acknowledgment is in the Power of Attorney, the Agent cannot claim ignorance regarding their fiduciary duties.

Article XV: Acknowledgment by the Agent

A: The Agent shall exercise due care and act in the Principal's best interest with the powers granted while adhering to any limitations, impositions, or specifications within this POA.

B: The Agent's foremost duty is loyalty and protection of the Principal and the Principal's interests. The Agent shall direct any benefits derived from this POA to the Principal. The Agent must avoid conflicts of interest and use ordinary skill and prudence to exercise these powers. If there is anything about this POA or the Agent's duties that the Agent does not understand, the Agent shall seek professional advice.

C: A court of competent jurisdiction has the discretion to revoke the Agent's power, especially if acting inappropriately. Thus, it behooves the Agent to exercise the bestowed powers in a fiduciary manner. The burden will be upon the Agent to prove that such acts were prudent and within a Fiduciary standard for any questionable acts. The Agent may be liable for damages and subject to criminal and civil prosecution if a court of competent jurisdiction finds that the Agent has violated their fiduciary duty.

D: The Agent has the power to abstain from using their granted powers under this POA; however, the Agent does not have the luxury of being negligent when the **Life, Safety**, and **Welfare** of the Principal are at stake. The Agent may be liable for damages, be subject to prosecution (criminal or civil), and suffer termination of powers if a court rules that the Agent has been negligent regarding their fiduciary duty under this POA to the Principal,

E: The Agent agrees to keep all monetary funds or financial assets that belong to the Principal in separate accounts from the Agent's monetary funds or financial assets. There shall be no commingling of monetary funds or financial assets to ensure simple accounting and safeguard the Principal's financial security. Furthermore, the Agent agrees to protect, conserve, and exercise prudence and caution in dealings with the Principal´s monetary funds, financial assets, and all other assets of value and worth.

F: The Agent agrees to keep a complete/accurate record of all acts, disbursements, and receipts for review/inspection. The Agent agrees to provide an accounting/report to the Principal at the following time intervals (as stated below). If the Principal dies, the Executor/Administrator of the Principal´s estate shall receive the accounting/report within a quarter. **Directions: Place a "✓" in the Accounting / Report Period box.**

Report Period: ☐ **None** ☐ **Monthly** ☐ **Quarterly** ☐ **Annually**

2

G: By default, the Agent shall not receive compensation for their authority, rights, and responsibilities; however, the Agent may receive reimbursement for reasonable and necessary expenses incurred in performing their authority, rights, and responsibilities. The Principal may compensate the Agent if the Principal desires.

H: The Agent shall disclose all actions that require written authorization by using their identity as the Agent in the following manner: (Agent's Signature) as Agent for (Principal's Name).

I: For Simple and Special POA, the Agent may resign by notifying the Principal or the Principal's Guardian or Conservator (provided a Judge appoints one). For Complex and Durable POA, the Agent may resign by notifying the Principal, Protector, Co-Agent, Successor Agent, or the Principal's Guardian or Conservator (provided a Judge appoints one). The resignation must be in writing and sent by certified mail, statutory overnight delivery (return receipt requested), or email.

J: If the Agent becomes aware of the death of the Principal who executed the POA, the Agent must notify all Third Parties as soon as practicable that the Principal has died and that this POA is no longer legitimate and effective. If Durability Provision(s) are not active or applicable, the Agent must notify all Third Parties as soon as practicable that the Principal is functioning non-socially, incapacitated, or incompetent; thus, the POA is no longer valid.

K: If the Agent resigns or ceases to represent the Principal regarding this POA, the former Agent agrees to return all property and documents to the Principal immediately.

Due to Space Limitations, Provisions L – R are not shown.

Built-in Safety Features

These documents come with **Built-in Safety Features** to protect the Principal; the following examples illustrate these safety features and explain why they exist.

Interpretation Instruction in the event of Ambiguities: It provides a set of rules to avoid litigation and determine the Principal intent if an error occurs.

Article XI: Ambiguities Interpretation Instructions

A: If a provision requires that a specific section be "Type" to be valid, failure to **"Type"** the section shall make that part invalid, null, and void.

B: If a provision requires that a specific section have the **Principal's Initial** for it to be valid, failure to initial the section shall make that part invalid, null, and void.

C: If a fillable section is **blank**, thus not typed or filled in, the legal interpretation shall be that the Principal did not intend for that section to be effective, and when it comes to interpreting that section, it shall be invalid, null, and void.

D: If a fillable section requires a **Yes "Y"** or **No "N"** and the section is blank (thus not typed or filled in), the legal interpretation shall be that the Principal did not intend for that section to be effective; therefore, it shall be **No** "N."

E: If a fillable section requires a **Yes "Y"** or **No "N;"** however, **"Yes"** or **"No"** exists instead, the legal interpretation shall be that the Principal did intend for that section to keep its legal effect and meaning.

F: If a fillable section requires a **Check "✓"** and it is blank, thus not typed or filled in, the legal interpretation shall be that the Principal did not intend for that section to be effective; therefore, not wanted.

G: If a fillable section gives multiple options that are mutually exclusive to each other in which a **Check "✓"** is required if more than one option is checked "✓" then the legal interpretation shall be that the Principal did this in error; thus when it comes to interpreting that section, the implementation shall be of the more conservative option.

H: If a fillable section requires a **Check "✓"** or "X," however a dash "—" exists instead, the legal interpretation shall be that the Principal did not intend for that section to be effective; thus, it is not wanted.

I: If a section or provision is typed with added handwritten instructions, only the "typed" section will receive consideration concerning the Principal's intentions. The rationale is simple: any person, not necessarily the Principal, can handwrite (ink in) after the fact. Due to a lack of verification, the additional handwritten instruction shall be invalid, null, and void.

J: Most state laws will void a legal document if someone writes on the surface, especially after notarization or execution. The Principal waives this right since the formalization of the POA requires it to be typed and printed; thus, any handwritten alteration concerning the altered section shall be unsubstantial and nonbearing unless an unaltered original duplicate or legitimate copy is available; only the unreadable section shall be invalid, null, and void,

K: If this POA allows handwritten statements by the Principal and there seem to be any suspicious alterations or additions (changes in handwriting style, changes in ink), such handwritten alterations or additions shall have no weight or bearing. Unless an unaltered original duplicate or legitimate copy is available, the altered section shall only be invalid, null, and void if it (the altered section) is unreadable as to its original intentions.

L: The Descriptions that follow a **Yes** "Y" or a **No** "N" Box are for clarification and informational purposes to outline the performance of duties and rights.

M: If a Third Party receives more than one active Power of Attorney regarding the Principal: **(01)** The Power of Attorney that has the most recent date shall take more precedence unless otherwise stated in **Article VII Subsection** G. **(02)** If the Principal function non-socially, incapacitated, or incompetent, then the Power of Attorney that has an active Durability Provision(s), in effect, shall take precedence. **(03)** If the Power of Attorney has the same date, then a General Power takes precedence over a Financial Power of Attorney. A Financial Power of Attorney takes precedence over a Banking Power of Attorney. A Limited Power of Attorney shall be subservient to a General, Financial, and Banking Power of Attorney if any conflicts arise. **(04)** A Protecting Power of Attorney shall stand alone and only be binding upon Complex and Durable Power of Attorney with active Protector provisions. **(05)** A Complex Power of Attorney takes precedence over a Simple Power of Attorney if any conflicts arise. **(06)** Unless otherwise specified within a Special Power of Attorney, a Special Power of Attorney shall take precedence over a Complex and Simple Power of Attorney if there are any conflicts.

Built-in Safety Features

These documents come with **Built-in Safety Features** to protect the Principal; the following examples illustrate these safety features and explain why they exist.

Witnesses and Notary Public Conflict of Interest: This Safety feature protects the Principal from conflict of interest and situations where the Principal's financial interest may be at stake.

*** None shall serve as a Witness, Notary Public, or other qualified individual with the authority to administer oaths regarding this POA made under this section.**

(**01**) Any individual related to the Principal by blood, marriage, or adoption. (**02**) Any individual currently a Beneficiary of the Principal's estate (laws of intestate succession or any existing will/codicil). (**03**) Any individual who benefits from a financial policy (insurance or annuity) in which the Principal's life is insured. (**04**) Any individual claiming (present/inchoate) any part of the Principal's estate. (**05**) Any individual who serves as an Owner, Operator, or employee of a Health Care Facility (Medical, Mental, or Assisted Living) in which the Principal is currently a Patient / Client unless the employee serves solely as a Notary Public. (**06**) Any Doctor, Physician, Psychologist, Psychiatrist, Social Worker, Financial Advisor, or Financial Manager in which the Principal is currently a Patient / Client. (**07**) Any individual who serves as an Owner, Operator, or employee of a Final Dispositional Facility (Funerary Home, Crematory Authority, and Cemetery Authority) unless the employee serves solely as a Notary Public. (**08**) Any individual who is an Agent (active/inactive) serving in a fiduciary capacity under this POA. (**09**) Upon the Principal's death, any individual or entity with a claim (the creditor) against the Principal's estate. (**10**) Any individual under eighteen (**18**) years or is incapacitated or incompetent. The Witnesses should be twenty-one (**21**) years of age or older.

Special Witness** If the Principal is a resident of a sanitarium, rest home, nursing home, boarding home, et cetera, it is highly beneficial that a patient advocate or ombudsman be one of the Witnesses while executing this POA. **Legal Questions:** Consult the State laws or contact a licensed Attorney.

This page is intentionally left blank

Optional Safety Features

Optional Safety Features

These documents come with **Optional Safety Features** to protect the Principal; the following example illustrates these safety features and their purpose.

Springing Powers: It allows the Principal to have such a document be active when said action or event occurs.

Article V: Springing Powers

SAFETY FEATURE: By implementing this option, the Principal creates an administrative burden but also creates checks and balances. This option is a personal decision that the Principal must determine for their future benefit. **STATEMENT OF ACKNOWLEDGMENT:** The Principal acknowledges and states that springing powers shall only occur if **Article III Option B** is active. Furthermore, the Principal dictates that one of the following scenarios below (if selected) shall transpire/occur to activate the Springing Powers of this POA.

DIRECTIONS: The Principal must **place "Y"** for **Yes in all applicable empty box spaces below and initial "✐" on the line** for activation of Springing Power(s). The Principal must **place "N"** for **No** to all applicable empty box spaces below **<u>and</u> initial "✐" the line** for no activation of Springing Power(s). Springing Power(s) will not receive activation if the empty box space or the Principal's initial is void or left blank.

"Y" or "N" Here ↑	Initial Here ↑	Scenario	Description
☐	____	**Incapacitation**	The Principal health state is **Incapacitation**; read **Article VI Subsection A**.
☐	____	**Incompetent**	The Principal health state is **Incompetent**; read **Article VI Subsection B** for more details.
☐	____	**Function Non-Socially**	The Principal health state is **Function Non-Socially**; read **Article VI Subsection C** for more details.
☐	____	**Active Duty – Overseas or Abroad**	The Principal is on **Active Duty either overseas or abroad** for a duration that lasts longer than (**07**) seven days (proof will consist of military orders or a signed, preferably notarized, letter from the Principal).
☐	____	**Business Trip – Overseas or Abroad**	The Principal is on a **business trip either overseas or abroad** for a duration that lasts longer than (**07**) seven days (proof will consist of a copy of the ticket purchased or a signed, preferably notarized, letter from the Principal).
☐	____	**Incarcerated in Jail, Prison, Correctional Facilities**	The Principal is in **jail, prison, or any other correctional facility** where freedom of personal movement is reduced or denied (proof will consist of evidence of incarceration or a signed, preferably notarized, letter from the Principal).
☐	____	**Recognize as being Officially Missing**	The Principal is officially missing (proof will consist of the missing person report by the government or law enforcement authority).

Due to Space Limitations, three (03) other scenarios are not shown.

Optional Safety Features

These documents come with **Optional Safety Features** to protect the Principal; the following example illustrates these safety features and why they exist.

Co-Power Sharing for Agent: It allows the Principal to designate an Agent to check and balance another Agent's action and vice versa due to an inherent lack of complete trust in a sole Agent.

Article VIII: Agent Co-Power Sharing

SAFETY FEATURE: Implementing this option creates an administrative burden, but it also creates checks and balances. This option is a personal decision that the Principal must make for their future benefit.

"Y" or "N" Here ↑ | Initial Here ↑

Place "Y" for Yes or "N" for No in the box and initial "✐" the line if the Principal desires the following:

Enable Agent Co-Power Sharing

By designating "Y" for Yes, the Principal has enabled co-power sharing for the Agent(s), which shall initially be the first and second choice Agent. The Agent(s) shall have the authority and power to make joint decisions on the Principal behalf in a co-power-sharing arrangement. Co-power sharing involves the Agent(s) making and implementing decisions together. Every joint decision must be in writing, with both Agents approving such decisions by signature. Succession for co-power sharing shall occur when an Agent is either unable or unwilling to accept or continue the appointment as the Agent; thus, the third choice as Agent shall take the place of the departing Agent. The succession for Agent shall continue in the manner above (as illustrated when the third choice for Agent assumes powers) until every named Agent is unable or unwilling to accept or continue the appointment as Agent. Furthermore, the Agents agree to perform all their duties as follows:

A: The Agents shall collaborate and share all knowledge and activities via letter, text, phone, or email. Email is the preferred method of communication.

B: The Agents shall not change the following: Account Information, Security Questions, Log-In Screen Name or I.D., and Passwords without having both active Agents agree to such changes in advance (preferably in writing email). An Agent shall be relieved of their powers/duties if an Agent initiates such changes to prevent the other Agent from knowing what activities are occurring.

C: Transparency is paramount, thus requiring continuous active support among all Agent(s). Disclosure of account status or changes must occur to all Agents within (07) seven days before activation or deactivation. Furthermore, all account information, security settings, and password information shall be up-to-date and continuously dispersed to all Agents (active) as soon as possible via the most efficient means of communication.

D: All Agents are accountable for their actions and shall not act alone without consent or prior agreement from the other Co-Agent; failure to do so may result in criminal or civil proceedings.

Resignation:	The Agent may resign by notifying the Principal, Protector (Complex & Durable POA), Co-Agent, Successor Agent, or the Principal's Guardian. The resignation must be in writing by certified mail, statutory overnight delivery (return receipt requested), or email.

Optional Safety Features

Only Complex and Durable Power of Attorneys come with **Optional Safety Features** to protect the Principal; the following example illustrates these safety features and their purpose.

Protector: It allows the Principal to designate a third party to monitor and record the Agent's actions. If the Principal has to resort to this level of oversight, this must be a last-resort option, with the Principal exhausting all other feasible options.

Article XII: Protector

SAFETY FEATURE: Implementing this option creates an administrative burden, but it also creates checks and balances. This option is a personal decision that the Principal must make for their future benefit.

"Y" or "N" Here ↑	Initial Here ↑	**Place "Y" for Yes or "N" for No in the box and initial "✐" the line if the Principal desires the following:**	**Restrict Agent's Powers by using a Protector**

By designating "Y" for Yes, the Principal has enacted a Durable Protecting Power of Attorney (DPPOA). The role of the Protector is to safeguard the best interest and wishes of the Principal, primarily in a passive capacity, and to provide basic administrative support to the Agent. However, when the Agent violates their role as a Fiduciary, it is the role of the Protector to step in, relieve the Agent, and protect the Principal's rights and interests.

The date of DPPOA Execution: **Month of:** ______ **Day of:** ______ **Year of:** ______

A formal recording/filing (optional) of the POA is with the following:

Public Records:			
Location:		**Docket #**	
Address:		**Page #**	

The Principal designates the Protector (the first choice) with decision-making powers to adhere to the terms within the DPPOA.

Protector 1st choice →				
Full Name:				
Address:				
Phone #:		**Email:**		
Residence:	**County:**		**State:**	

In the unlikely event that the Protector (the first choice) refuses, is unable, or is denied (by a Judge or Principal) to act as a Protector. The Principal designates the successor Protector (the second choice) with decision-making powers to adhere to the terms within the DPPOA.

Protector 2nd choice →				
Full Name:				
Address:				
Phone #:		**Email:**		
Residence:	**County:**		**State:**	

In the unlikely event that the Protector (the second choice) refuses, is unable, or is denied (by a Judge or Principal) to act as a Protector. The Principal dictates that a court of legal jurisdiction shall appoint a Protector for the Principal with decision-making powers to adhere to the terms within the DPPOA.

A: An active Protector shall not serve as an acting Agent; this is to prevent a conflict of interest. The individual must either abstain or resign from one of the roles to perform the functions of the other.

B: The Protector (listed above) must be an Agent within the DPPOA to have power over the POA's Agents. The choice selection for Protector may not be in the same order as shown on the POA; if there is a conflict regarding choice selection designation, the POA shall take precedence.

Optional Safety Features

These documents come with **Optional Safety Features** to protect the Principal; the following example illustrates these safety features and explains why they exist.

Durability Provisions: This provision allows the Principal to "put in stone" per se the Agent's ability to continue to act on the Principal's behalf if the Principal were to suffer Incompetence, Incapacity, or Functioning Non-Socially in the future.

Article XIII: Durability Provisions

Statement of Understanding by the Principal: The Principal understands that the direction and choices implemented by the Agent as specified in this POA (if still active due to durability provision(s) and not previously revoked) shall continue, even if the Principal objects to the actions or decisions later when the Principal is functioning non-socially, incapacitated, or incompetent.

DIRECTIONS: The Principal must **place "Y"** for **Yes in all applicable empty box spaces below and initial "✎" on the line** for activation of Durable Power(s). The Principal must **place "N"** for **No** to all applicable empty box spaces below **and initial "✎" the line** for no activation of Durable Power(s). Durable Power(s) will not receive activation if the empty box space or the Principal's initial is void or left blank.

"Y" or "N" Here ↑	Initial Here ↑	**Place "Y" for Yes or "N" for No in the box and initial "✎" the line if the Principal desires the following:**	**(A)**	**Durability against Incompetence**

DESCRIPTION: By designating "Y" for Yes, this POA shall continue if the Principal becomes incompetent; this POA shall survive the effects of incompetence and shall not be invalid, null, or void. Furthermore, the Agent's power and authority shall remain effective when the Principal is incompetent.

"Y" or "N" Here ↑	Initial Here ↑	**Place "Y" for Yes or "N" for No in the box and initial "✎" the line if the Principal desires the following:**	**(B)**	**Durability against Incapacity**

DESCRIPTION: By designating "Y" for Yes, this POA shall continue if the Principal becomes incapacitated; this POA shall survive the effects of incapacity and shall not be invalid, null, or void. Furthermore, the Agent's power and authority shall remain effective when the Principal is incapacitated.

"Y" or "N" Here ↑	Initial Here ↑	**Place "Y" for Yes or "N" for No in the box and initial "✎" the line if the Principal desires the following:**	**(C)**	**Durability against Functioning Non-Socially**

DESCRIPTION: By designating "Y" for Yes, this POA shall continue if the Principal functions Non-Socially; this POA shall survive the effects of functioning non-socially and shall not be invalid, null, or void. Furthermore, the Agent's power and authority shall remain effective when the Principal functions non-socially.

Recommendation:	The Agent should attach the **Affidavit of Principal's Health State** by a licensed Health Professional (dated before the expiration date) if the Principal is functioning non-socially, incapacitated, or incompetent when presenting the POA to any Third Party.

Optional Safety Features

These documents come with **Optional Safety Features** to protect the Principal; the following example illustrates these safety features and their purpose.

Require the Utilization of "Acknowledgment of Appointment by Agent": Require the Agent to sign off on the "Acknowledgment of Appointment by Agent" form before allowing the perspective Agent to act as the Principal's Agent. This would allow for greater accountability for the Agent's actions if litigation were to occur.

Article XVI: Acknowledgment of Appointment by the Agent

SAFETY FEATURE: Implementing this option creates an administrative burden, but it also creates checks and balances. This option is a personal decision that the Principal must make for their future benefit.

Place "Y" for Yes or "N" for No in the box and initial "✎" the line if the Principal desires the following:

Requires Utilization of Acknowledgment of Appointment by Agent Form

"Y" or "N" Here ↑ Initial Here ↑

For brevity and consistency, the abbreviation of "**Acknowledgment of Appointment by Agent**" shall be "**Appointment.**" By designating "Y" for Yes, the Principal must fill out, sign, and notarize the Appointment as a condition of becoming the acting Agent. The Agent shall forfeit their right to serve as an Agent by default if the Agent fails to implement the Appointment. The successor Agent shall become the current acting Agent, provided the successor Agent executes the Appointment. The appointment shall become a prerequisite for the Agent to implement in all succession matters. If the Principal selects a Co-Power Sharing for Agents, implementing this Appointment shall still be a requirement for each Agent. When utilizing the POA with any Third Party, the Agent shall provide a copy of the Appointment to the Third Party. Failure to provide a copy of the Appointment to the Third Party shall result in the Third Party refusing and declining the POA.

Article XVIII: Authorization of Delegation of Agent's Power to another Agent

SAFETY FEATURE: Implementing this option creates an administrative burden, but it also creates checks and balances. This option is a personal decision that the Principal must make for their future benefit.

Place "Y" for Yes or "N" for No in the box and initial "✎" the line if the Principal desires the following:

Delegation of Agent's Powers to another Agent

"Y" or "N" Here ↑ Initial Here ↑

By designating "Y" for Yes, the Principal allows delegating an Agent's powers to another Agent in **Article VII**. This discretionary power is useful when the acting Agent suffers inconveniences due to a lack of knowledge, logistics issues, or time constraints. The Agent who receives power from another Agent is the "Delegate." For transparency and record-keeping purposes, the utilization of the following forms shall occur: "**Delegation of Agent's Powers**" and "**Revocation of Delegate by (Agent, Principal, or Protector)**" with a copy mailed by the Agent to the Principal. If the Principal revokes an Agent, and the Agent has a Delegate, then the Delegate's powers are no longer active. If the Principal or Protector revokes an Agent due to a violation of Fiduciary duties, then that Agent shall not serve in the future as a Delegate. If the Principal or Protector revokes a Delegate for violating Fiduciary duties, then that Delegate shall not serve as an Agent forever.

Optional Safety Features

These documents come with **Optional Safety Features** to protect the Principal; the following example illustrates these safety features and their purpose.

Security Footer Setting: This ensures the document's legitimacy, thus making it extremely difficult to forge or tamper with this POA from interested parties.

Article XIX: Security Footer Setting

SAFETY FEATURE: To prevent fraud and ensure legitimacy, the Principal may desire to enact a security feature known as the "**Security Footer**." Security Footer is burdensome; however, if the Principal believes that a party will contest or illegitimately alter this POA, selecting the "High" setting may be desirable. The following pages will not usually have a security feature: (**01**) Cover Page, (**02**) Table of Contents, (**03**) Warning Page, (**04**) Informational Page, and (**05**) Intentionally blank separate page. The Principal requires the POA to have the following security setting: **Directions: Place a "✓" in the Security Level box.**

Security Level: ☐ None ☐ Low ☐ Moderate ☐ High

If the security selection is "**None**," no initial on the Security Footer is required. If the security selection is "**Low**," then the Principal's initial is required in the Security Footer. If the security selection is "**Moderate**," then the Principal's and Notary's initials are required in the Security Footer. If the security selection is "**High**," then the Principal's, Notary's, and Witness's initial is required in the Security Footer. The default option is "None" if the security selection is left blank (not "✓").

A: It might be suspicious if a page within this POA lacks the necessary initials, as stated in the Security Footer setting indicated above. In this event, the whole page shall be invalid and deemed unenforceable.

B: If a Witness but not the other Witness (when (**02**) two Witnesses are required) forgot to initial the Security Footer, but the Notary and Principal initial that page, then that page shall survive **Article XIX, Subsection A**. However, if no Notary's initial is present in the Security Footer and the Witness's initial is missing, then that page shall be subject to **Article XIX, Subsection A.**

C: Under State Law, if this POA is valid and enforceable with a Security Footer level of "Moderate," even though it is supposed to have a "High" Security Footer level." Then the following shall apply: If one or both Witnesses do not initial the Security Footer even though the Security Footer level is "High," then that page shall survive **Article XIX, Subsection A**, providing that the Principal and Notary have initialed the page.

D: If the Security Footer requires a Notary's Initial and the Notary's Initial is not present, the page shall be subject to **Article XIX, Subsection A.**

E: If the Security Footer requires a Principal's Initial and the Principal's Initial is not present, the page shall be subject to **Article XIX, Subsection A.**

F: If a Witness is also a potential Health Care Surrogate, Mental Health Care Surrogate, Agent, Guardian, or Conservator, then due to conflict of interest, the Witness shall not serve in such a fiduciary capacity unless the Witness gets approval through a court of competent jurisdiction to act in a fiduciary role.

G: To prevent fraud, every revocation requires a Notary Initial, Signature, and Seal; one or more Witnesses are not required.

This page is intentionally left blank

CHAPTER 03

CHAPTER

03

Complex Financial Power of Attorney

CHAPTER 03

Overview

CHAPTER

03

Complex Financial Power of Attorney

Overview

It is highly advantageous that the Principal trusts the person acting as their Agent completely for the Complex Financial Power of Attorney. That person shall have power over the Principal assets and affairs as if the Principal were there in person.

This Power of Attorney is "**Complex**" for the following reasons: (**01**) It names multiple Agents with successors Agent. (**02**) The effective date or expiration date may be contingent upon multiple variables. (**03**) There are springing, and sprinkling powers added. (**04**) Durable provisions are optional. (**05**) Multiple safety features are available; however, implementation is optional.

- **Complex Financial Power of Attorney (CFPOA) (22 Pages Total)**
  Only utilize this document if necessary and in a prudent manner. This Power of Attorney gives the Agent the powers to handle financial activities and perform financial transactions. **Please Note:** There is no need to fill out a Complex Banking Power of Attorney if the Principal enacts a Complex Financial Power of Attorney.

Complex Financial Power of Attorney

Complex Financial Power of Attorney

Objective:

The objective of this Complex Financial Power of Attorney (CFPOA) is to give the individual whom the Principal has designated as the Agent the power and ability to do the following transactions on the Principal's behalf: **(A) Banking / Financial Institution Transactions; (B) Access to Safe Deposit Box or Vaults; (C) Payment Transactions; (D) Borrowing Transactions; (E) Accounts Receivable Transactions; (F) Insurance and Annuity Transactions; (G) Financial Securities; (H) Commodity, Futures, and Options; (I) Benefits - Governmental / Civilian Programs; (J) Tax Returns, Reports, and Transactions; (K) Legal - Litigation, Claims, & Disputes; (L) Hiring Representatives; (M) Estate, Trust, and other Beneficiary Transactions; (N) Retirement Plan or Benefit Transactions; and (O) Other Terms: (Conditions, Prohibitions, Restriction, Exceptions, Additions, Limitation, Extensions, Special Rules)**. This Power of Attorney is complex for the following reasons: (**01**) It names multiple Agents with the successor's Agent. (**02**) The effective or expiration date may be contingent upon multiple variables. (**03**) Springing and sprinkling powers were added. (**04**) Durable provision(s) are optional. (**05**) Multiple safety features are available; however, implementation is optional.

Do The Following:

Please note that the possibility exists that transactions or third parties may not permit using this CFPOA; suggest checking for unusual requirements or imposition in advance. The Principal should know that most financial institutions or businesses would only honor a durable power of attorney. Usually, vetting of the power of attorneys must occur first in the legal department before utilization due to liability reasons. Upon filling out the CFPOA, print off at least (**03**) three copies, (**01**) one for each of the following: Principal, Agent, and each financial institution or business. Please note that the possibility exists that financial institutions or businesses will only honor a power of attorney of their own making; thus, the Agent may have to sue to enforce a power of attorney. Other financial institutions or businesses may have policies requiring the account holder to provide a power of attorney in person for their "folder" before utilization. Most financial institutions or businesses will not accept a Non-Durable Power of Attorney.

Not A Court Order:

Please Note: This is not a court order. Executing this CFPOA is strictly voluntary. Implementing the CFPOA must be proactive to be effective and valid. It is highly advantageous that the Principal record/file (optional) the CFPOA with the courts or county clerk. Falsification of this CFPOA may constitute a criminal offense.

Note of Caution:

When filling out this CFPOA, please consider the following. The Purchaser or User should seek a legal professional's advice if the Purchaser or User is less than eighteen (18) years of age and currently deemed mentally incompetent or incapacitated. Feel free to utilize this CFPOA as a template. However, without legal representation in the situation above, this CFPOA would suffer litigation by Interested Third Parties and more than likely receive judgment as invalid. Remember, an active lawful court order covering the subject matter within this CFPOA will always take precedence if a conflict occurs. **Please Note:** If the Purchaser or User does have an active court order. The Purchaser or User can design this CFPOA, so it is not in conflict; however, seek the advice of a legal professional if there are any questions.

Complex Financial Power of Attorney

Table of Contents:

Helpful Suggestions / Recommendations:

- Most notaries who notarize a document for free as part of their occupation will usually only notarize one document versus having multiple originals. **Recommendation:** Find out what the Notary will do in advance.
- Keep the Original CFPOA in a safe place (preferably a fireproof vault or safe) and give an original copy to a trusted individual.
- Make multiple copies of this CFPOA. Give a copy to each interested Third Party. Maintain a list of who has copies of this CFPOA in their procession. Attach the list to the Original CFPOA in the Principal procession. If the CFPOA is revoked, refer to the list to retrieve the CFPOA in question.
- The easiest way to restrict this CFPOA is to establish an Expiration Date, preferably in five (**05**) to ten (**10**) year increments. Upon expiration of this CFPOA, the Principal will have to execute a new CFPOA to continue the agency relationship regarding the Principal's property and affairs.
- The Principal should execute an Affidavit of Principal's Health State by a licensed Health Professional if there are questions or doubts regarding the Principal's capacity, competence, or social functionality. Attach the executed Affidavit of Principal's Health State to the Original CFPOA. If applicable, give a trusted individual an original copy of the Affidavit of Principal's Health State.

Complex Financial Power of Attorney

Important Document

- Before signing this Complex Financial Power of Attorney (CFPOA), the Principal should know these important facts. This CFPOA aims to give the individual the Principal designates as their "Agent" **powers to handle financial activities and perform financial transactions during the Principal's lifetime**. These powers may include the following: **(A) Banking / Financial Institution Transactions; (B) Access to Safe Deposit Box or Vaults; (C) Payment Transactions; (D) Borrowing Transactions; (E) Accounts Receivable Transactions; (F) Insurance and Annuity Transactions; (G) Financial Securities; (H) Commodity, Futures, and Options; (I) Benefits - Governmental / Civilian Programs; (J) Tax Returns, Reports, and Transactions; (K) Legal - Litigation, Claims, & Disputes; (L) Hiring Representatives; (M) Estate, Trust, and other Beneficiary Transactions; (N) Retirement Plan or Benefit Transactions; and (O) Other Terms: (Conditions, Prohibitions, Restriction, Exceptions, Additions, Limitation, Extensions, Special Rules).**
- **Please Note:** While the Principal is competent, the Principal still has all the power and rights to control their property and affairs as the Principal deems fit, despite any powers the Principal may have bestowed.
- The Principal must talk to their Agent often, specifically about what the Agent does while using this CFPOA. If the Agent is not following the Principal's written instructions, the Principal may revoke this CFPOA or end the Agent's powers.
- **Beware:** Please note that the possibility exists that Third Parties or certain transactions may not permit the use of this CFPOA; it is advisable to check in advance, if possible, for any special requirements or imposition.
- This CFPOA does not impose a duty on the Agent to exercise discretionary powers. However, when using these powers, the Agent must use due care to act for the Principal's benefit and adhere to this CFPOA. The Agent must act consistently with the Principal's desires, as stated in the CFPOA. Unless the Principal says or limits otherwise, the Agent has the same level of authority to make decisions. **Please Note:** A court could take away the powers of an Agent if the Agent authorizes anything that is illegal or acts contrary to this CFPOA.
- The Agent may exercise these powers throughout the Principal's lifetime unless otherwise limited in writing (time duration or event occurrence). Furthermore, these powers will continue to exist and shall be enforceable (if the durable provision(s) are active) if the Principal develops one or more of the following: (**01**) have a disability that renders the Principal to function non-socially. (**02**) The Principal is incapacitated. (**03**) The Principal is incompetent.
- This CFPOA does not authorize anyone to make health care decisions for the Principal. The Principal should implement the following if the Principal wishes to have health care decisions made: (**01**) Advanced Medical Health Directive, (**02**) Advanced Mental Health Directive, (**03**) Do Not Resuscitate Advance Directive (DNR), (**04**) Durable Power of Attorney for Health Care, (**05**) Declaration of Health Care (Living Will), and (**06**) Declaration of Organs & Tissues Donation (Anatomical Gifts).
- This CFPOA does not authorize anyone to decide guardianship regarding a minor or a disabled adult; neither gives the Agent the right to delegate Parental or Guardian authority. The Principal should implement the following if the Principal wishes to delegate their Parental / Guardian authority: (**01**) Simple or Complex Power of Attorney for Minor Child. (**02**) Durable Power of Attorney for Health Care of Minor Child. (**03**) Declaration of Guardianship & Conservatorship for Minor Child. (**04**) Declaration of Guardianship & Conservatorship for the Disabled.
- This CFPOA does not authorize anyone to decide guardianship or conservatorship regarding the Principal, nor does it give the Agent's powers of delegation regarding the Guardian or Conservator authority. If the Principal wishes to establish a Guardian or Conservator, the Principal should implement the following: (**01**) Declaration of Guardianship & Conservatorship.
- The creation and design of this CFPOA require no legal assistance to complete. The Principal or Agent should seek advice from a licensed Attorney for clarification or questions regarding this CFPOA.
- The Principal may revoke this CFPOA if the Principal is competent. The Principal should contact a licensed Attorney if the Agent continues to act after the Principal has revoked the Agent's powers and notified the Agent of their termination. Should the Principal revoke the Agent's authority, a written Revocation should be hand-delivered or mailed to where this CFPOA has been utilized.
- Use this CFPOA only after careful consideration. The Principals' execution and implementation of this CFPOA should be free from pressure. Do not name an Agent or grant power unless it is the Principal's choice.

Complex Financial Power of Attorney

Article I: Creation Statement

The Principal (stated below) revokes every previous Complex Financial Power of Attorney with an execution date predating this document.

Principal →

Full Name: ______________________

Address: ______________________

Phone #: __________ **Email:** __________

Residence: **County:** __________ **State:** __________

The Principal affirms the following in the Witnesses and Notary presence: (**01**) The Principal is at least eighteen (**18**) years or older. (**02**) The Principal is of sound and disposing mind (emotionally and mentally competent) to make or request this Complex Financial Power of Attorney. (**03**) The Principal has the capacity with full memory or necessary mental faculties to understand and comprehend these actions. (**04**) The Principal willfully and voluntarily executes this Complex Financial Power of Attorney. The following abbreviations shall be used for brevity and consistency: Complex Financial **Power of Attorney** shall be "**CFPOA**," and Attorney-In-Fact shall be "**Agent**."

Article II: Purpose

As stated in **Article VII**, The Principal appoints, authorizes, and designates the following Agent to make decisions and perform actions for the Principal according to the CFPOA terms and conditions as indicated in **Article III** through **Article XX**.

Article III: Effective Date of CFPOA

The Principal wants the following regarding the effective date for the legal enforcement of this CFPOA: The Principal can choose from (**02**) two options; however, **options A** and **B** are mutually exclusive. **Option A** shall be the default option in the event of ambiguities.

[ ] "Y" or "N" Here ↑ ________ Initial Here ↑

Place "Y" for Yes or "N" for No in the box and initial "✎" the line if the Principal desires the following:

(A) Effective Immediately

By designating "Y" for Yes, the effective date of this CFPOA shall begin from the day of execution, as stated in **Article XX**. If durability provision(s) are active in **Article XIII**, those provision(s) shall immediately take effect.

[ ] "Y" or "N" Here ↑ ________ Initial Here ↑

Place "Y" for Yes or "N" for No in the box and initial "✎" the line if the Principal desires the following:

(B) Effective if Events are Trigger

By designating "Y" for Yes, the effective date of this CFPOA shall begin when such events transpire or occur, as outlined in **Article V**: "**Springing Powers.**" If durability provision(s) are active in **Article XIII**, the durability provision(s) shall be active when such events transpire, as outlined in **Article V**: "**Springing Powers.**"

Article IV: Expiration Date of CFPOA

The Principal wants the following regarding the expiration date for the legal enforcement of this CFPOA: The Principal can choose from (**02**) two options; however, **options A** and **B** are mutually exclusive. **Option B** shall be the default option in the event of ambiguities.

[ ] "Y" or "N" Here ↑ ________ Initial Here ↑

Place "Y" for Yes or "N" for No in the box and initial "✎" the line if the Principal desires the following:

(A) Expire by a Define Date

By designating "Y" for Yes, the Principal wants to establish an expiration date for this CFPOA as stated below.

The date that CFPOA Expires: **Month of:** ______ **Day of:** ______ **Year of:** ______

"Y" or "N" Here ↑ Initial Here ↑

Place "Y" for Yes or "N" for No in the box and initial "✐" the line if the Principal desires the following:

(B) Expire by Revocation

By designating "Y" for Yes, the expiration date of this CFPOA shall end when the Principal revokes this CFPOA while in a Healthy state or other methods as outlined in **Article XI Subsection B.**

Article V: Springing Powers

SAFETY FEATURE: By implementing this option, the Principal creates an administrative burden but also creates checks and balances. This option is a personal decision that the Principal must determine for their future benefit. **STATEMENT OF ACKNOWLEDGMENT:** The Principal acknowledges and states that springing powers shall only occur if **Article III Option B** is active. Furthermore, the Principal dictates that one of the following scenarios below (if selected) shall transpire/occur to activate the Springing Powers of this CFPOA.

DIRECTIONS: The Principal must **place "Y"** for **Yes in all applicable empty box spaces below and initial "✐" on the line** for activation of Springing Power(s). The Principal must **place "N"** for **No** to all applicable empty box spaces below **and initial "✐" the line** for no activation of Springing Power(s). Springing Power(s) will not receive activation if the empty box space or the Principal's initial is void or left blank.

"Y" or "N" Here ↑ Initial Here ↑

Incapacitation

The Principal health state is **Incapacitation**; read **Article VI Subsection A**.

"Y" or "N" Here ↑ Initial Here ↑

Incompetent

The Principal health state is **Incompetent**; read **Article VI Subsection B** for more details.

"Y" or "N" Here ↑ Initial Here ↑

Function Non-Socially

The Principal health state is **Function Non-Socially**; read **Article VI Subsection C** for more details.

"Y" or "N" Here ↑ Initial Here ↑

Active Duty – Overseas or Abroad

The Principal is on **Active Duty either overseas or abroad** for a duration that lasts longer than **(07)** seven days (proof will consist of military orders or a signed, preferably notarized, letter from the Principal).

"Y" or "N" Here ↑ Initial Here ↑

Business Trip – Overseas or Abroad

The Principal is on a **business trip either overseas or abroad** for a duration that lasts longer than **(07)** seven days (proof will consist of a copy of the ticket purchased or a signed, preferably notarized, letter from the Principal).

"Y" or "N" Here ↑ Initial Here ↑

Incarcerated in Jail, Prison, Correctional Facilities

The Principal is in **jail, prison, or any other correctional facility** where freedom of personal movement is reduced or denied (proof will consist of evidence of incarceration or a signed, preferably notarized, letter from the Principal).

"Y" or "N" Here ↑ Initial Here ↑

Recognize as being Officially Missing

The Principal is officially missing (proof will consist of the missing person report by the government or law enforcement authority).

"Y" or "N" Here ↑	Initial Here ↑	**Homestead is uninhabitable or lost**	The Principal **Homestead is uninhabitable or lost** due to a natural disaster or other causes (proof will consist of one or more of the following: an insurance report or estimate, an inspector's report, or a report by a government or law enforcement authority).
"Y" or "N" Here ↑	Initial Here ↑	**Medical or Mental Health Institution / Facility**	The Principal has been in the custodial care of a Medical or Mental Health Institution/Facility for more than (**07**) seven days (proof will consist of evidence of stay at a Mental Health Institution/Facility or a signed, preferably notarized, letter from the Principal).
"Y" or "N" Here ↑	Initial Here ↑	**Kidnapped, held for ransom, sold into slavery, serfdom, sexual servitude, or unfree labor**	The Principal is **kidnapped, held for ransom, sold into slavery, serfdom, sexual servitude, or unfree labor** (proof will consist of a statement or report by the government or law enforcement authority or a verifiable and credible ransom demand or ransom letter).

Article VI: Health Status Definitions

A: Incapacitation shall occur if a court of competent jurisdiction has issued a court order stating that the Principal is incapacitated. Alternatively, the Principal currently has a medical and mental health condition diagnosed by (**02**) two licensed independent Physicians who have personally examined the Principal. Under the penalty of perjury, the Physicians stated in writing that the Principal demonstrates one or more of the following conditions. (**01**) The Principal cannot make, participate, or communicate a decision regarding their health care. (**02**) The Principal cannot manage the following: their care, property, or financial affairs. When trying to conceptualize what an incapacitated individual can do, think of an individual unable to control their motor movement and needing help to do regular tasks. Examples include (but are not limited to) the following: Amyotrophic Lateral Sclerosis (ALS), Primary Lateral Sclerosis (PLS), Progressive Bulbar Palsy (PBP), Progressive Muscular Atrophy (PMA), Pseudobulbar Palsy, and Parkinson's disease.

B: Incompetent shall occur if a court of competent jurisdiction has issued a court order stating that the Principal is incompetent. Alternatively, the Principal currently has a medical and mental health condition with diagnosis by (**02**) two independent Licensed Health Professionals (any combination will do) that serve in the following capacity (Physician, Clinical Psychologist, or Psychiatrist) who has personally examined the Principal. In writing, the Health Professionals state that the Principal demonstrates one or more of the following under the penalty of perjury. (**01**) The Principal cannot understand and appreciate the extent, nature, and probable consequences of a proposed medical and mental health decision that may or may not have life-sustaining implications. (**02**) The Principal cannot make an informed, intelligent decision in a reasonable amount of time. (**03**) The Principal cannot communicate a coherent decision no matter how simple the communication process is. (**04**) The Principal cannot rationally evaluate the risks and benefits of a proposed medical and mental health decision compared to the risks and benefits of alternatives. Examples include (but are not limited to) the following: Alzheimer's disease, Huntington's disease, Schizophrenia, Psychotic Disorder, and Severe Dementia. **Please Note:** An individual with a mental illness, advanced age, or developmental disability does not automatically imply or constitute a lack of decisional capacity.

C: Function Non-Socially shall occur if a court of competent jurisdiction has issued a court order stating that the Principal is functioning non-socially. Alternatively, the Principal currently has a medical and mental health condition diagnosed by (**02**) two licensed independent Physicians who have personally examined the Principal. The Physicians stated in writing, under the penalty of perjury, that the Principal cannot demonstrate one or more of the following: to recognize people, communicate with people, and interact with people in a meaningful way.

D: By the term **Healthy**, the Principal means the following: exhibit capacity with complete mental competence, thus fully capable of independent thought and actions, and function socially.

Article VII: Designation of Agent

The Principal should only designate an Agent if that individual is **Reliable**, **Trustworthy**, and **Competent** to manage the Principal's affairs. For legal reasons, all Agents must be competent and at least eighteen (**18**) years or older. None of the following individuals (non-relative) may serve as the Principal's Agent. (**A**) Any individual who serves as an Owner, Operator, or employee of a Health Care Facility (Medical, Mental, or Assisted Living) in which the Principal is currently a Patient / Client unless the employee serves solely as a Notary Public. (**B**) Any individual who serves as an Owner, Operator, or employee of a Final Dispositional Facility (Funerary Home, Crematory Authority, and Cemetery Authority) unless the employee serves solely as a Notary Public. (**C**) Any Doctor, Physician, Psychologist, Psychiatrist, Social Worker, Financial Advisor, or Financial Manager in which the Principal is currently a Patient / Client. Automatic Revocation of the Spouse designation as Agent shall occur if the following happens: (**01**) Dissolution or annulment of the marriage. (**02**) Proceedings are currently active for Dissolution of Marriage. (**03**) The Principal currently lives in a separate physical location from their Spouse for more than (**02**) two months with the intention of a divorce. The Principal designates the following individual as the Agent, the first choice, with decision-making powers in adherence to the terms and conditions specified in this CFPOA.

AGENT 1st choice →				
Full Name:				
Address:				
Phone #:		**Email:**		
Residence:	**County:**		**State:**	

In the unlikely event that the Agent (the first choice) refuses, is unable, or is denied (by a Judge or Principal) to act as an Agent. The Principal designates the successor Agent (the second choice) with decision-making powers to adhere to the terms and conditions specified in this CFPOA.

AGENT 2nd choice →				
Full Name:				
Address:				
Phone #:		**Email:**		
Residence:	**County:**		**State:**	

In the unlikely event that the Agent (the second choice) refuses, is unable, or is denied (by a Judge or Principal) to act as an Agent. The Principal designates the successor Agent (the third choice) with decision-making powers to adhere to the terms and conditions specified in this CFPOA.

AGENT 3rd Choice →				
Full Name:				
Address:				
Phone #:		**Email:**		
Residence:	**County:**		**State:**	

In the unlikely event that the Agent (the third choice) refuses, is unable, or is denied (by a Judge or Principal) to act as an Agent. The Principal designates the successor Agent (the fourth choice) with decision-making powers to adhere to the terms and conditions specified in this CFPOA.

AGENT 4th Choice →				
Full Name:				
Address:				
Phone #:		**Email:**		
Residence:	**County:**		**State:**	

In the unlikely event that the Agent (the fourth choice) refuses, is unable, or is denied (by a Judge or Principal) to act as an Agent. The Principal designates the successor Agent (the fifth choice) with decision-making powers to adhere to the terms and conditions specified in this CFPOA.

AGENT 5th Choice →				
Full Name:				
Address:				
Phone #:		**Email:**		
Residence:	**County:**		**State:**	

In the unlikely event that the Agent (the fifth choice) refuses, is unable, or is denied (by a Judge or Principal) to act as an Agent. The Principal dictates that a court of legal jurisdiction shall appoint an Agent for the Principal to act in adherence to the terms of the CFPOA.

Article VIII: Agent Co-Power Sharing

SAFETY FEATURE: Implementing this option creates an administrative burden, but it also creates checks and balances. This option is a personal decision that the Principal must make for their future benefit.

[ ]	______	**Place "Y" for Yes or "N" for No in the box and initial "🖉" the line if the Principal desires the following:**	**Enable Agent Co-Power Sharing**
"Y" or "N" Here ↑	**Initial Here ↑**		

By designating "Y" for Yes, the Principal has enabled co-power sharing for the Agent(s), which shall initially be the first and second choice Agent. The Agent(s) shall have the authority and power to make joint decisions on the Principal's behalf in a co-power-sharing arrangement. Co-power sharing involves the Agent(s) making and implementing decisions together. Every joint decision must be in writing, with both Agents approving such decisions by signature. Succession for co-power sharing shall occur when an Agent is either unable or unwilling to accept or continue the appointment as the Agent; thus, the third choice as Agent shall take the place of the departing Agent. The succession for Agent shall continue in the manner above (as illustrated when the third choice for Agent assumes powers) until every named Agent is unable or unwilling to accept or continue the appointment as Agent. Furthermore, the Agents agree to perform all their duties as follows:

A: The Agents shall collaborate and share all knowledge and activities via letter, text, phone, or email. Email is the preferred method of communication.

B: The Agents shall not change the following: Account Information, Security Questions, Log-In Screen Name or I.D., and Passwords without having both active Agents agree to such changes in advance (preferably in writing email). An Agent shall be relieved of their powers/duties if an Agent initiates such changes to prevent the other Agent from knowing what activities are occurring.

C: Transparency is paramount, thus requiring continuous active support among all Agent(s). Disclosure of account status or changes must occur to all Agents within (07) seven days before activation or deactivation. Furthermore, all account information, security settings, and password information shall be up-to-date and continuously dispersed to all Agents (active) as soon as possible via the most efficient means of communication.

D: All Agents are accountable for their actions and shall not act alone without consent or prior agreement from the other Co-Agent; failure to do so may result in criminal or civil proceedings.

Resignation:	The Agent may resign by notifying the Principal, Protector (Complex & Durable POA), Co-Agent, Successor Agent, or the Principal's Guardian. The resignation must be in writing by certified mail, statutory overnight delivery (return receipt requested), or email.

Article IX: Powers, Rights, Privileges

Statement from the Principal to the Third Parties: All Third Parties dealing in good faith with the Agent may fully rely upon the Agent's power and authority to act on the Principal's behalf and in the Principal's name. All Third Parties may accept and rely on agreements and other instruments entered or executed by the Agent under this CFPOA.

Power and Authority to Acts: The Agent's powers include the ability to act in the Principal name, place, and stead in any way (in parts or whole) that is proper and prudent. The Agent's powers include acting to the fullest and greatest extent possible in which the Principal is permissible by law to act through an Agent with the Principal's best interest and welfare in mind.

The Agent's Powers: The Agent shall have the full power and authority to exercise, perform, manage, and conduct in a fiduciary capacity and shall act with utmost good faith, fair dealing, full disclosure, and fidelity towards the Principal. The Agent shall have any incidental rights required to conduct and perform the specific powers granted herein. The Agent shall exercise the Principal legal rights and powers, including those rights and powers that the Principal may acquire in the future.

DIRECTIONS: The Principal must **place "Y"** for **Yes** in all applicable empty box spaces below and initial "🖉" on **the line** for activation of Agent's Power(s). The Principal must **place "N"** for **No** to all applicable empty box spaces below **and initial "🖉" the line** for no activation of Agent's Power(s). Agent's Power(s) will not receive activation if the empty box space or the Principal's initial is void or left blank.

"Y" or "N" Here ↑ Initial Here ↑

Place "Y" for Yes or "N" for No in the box and initial "✐" the line if the Principal desires the following:

(A) Banking / Financial Institution Transactions

DESCRIPTION: By designating "Y" for Yes, the Agent's powers include the ability to do the following regarding **Banking / Financial Institution Transactions**: **(01)** to open, close, accept, continue, and control all accounts and deposits. **(02)** To make, demand, recover, receive, sign, stop, endorse, execute, acknowledge, deliver, and possess checks, drafts, bills of exchange, letters of credit, certificates of deposit, notes, stock certificates, warrants, withdrawal receipts, deposit instruments, and other negotiable paper. **(03)** To withdraw and deposit funds (by check or withdrawal slips) that the Principal has on deposit (now or in the future) from any financial institution. The financial institution includes, without limitation, banks, trust companies, associations (savings, building, and loan), credit unions, and brokerage firms.

"Y" or "N" Here ↑ Initial Here ↑

Place "Y" for Yes or "N" for No in the box and initial "✐" the line if the Principal desires the following:

(B) Access to Safe-Deposit Box/Vaults

DESCRIPTION: By designating "Y" for Yes, the Agent's powers include the ability to do the following regarding **Access to Safe-Deposit Boxes or Vaults**: **(01)** to open, continue, and have free access at any time to any safety deposit boxes/vaults registered in the Principal name alone or jointly with others. **(02)** To remove any property or papers therein; sign, renew, release, or terminate any safe deposit contract; drill or surrender any safe-deposit boxes/vaults.

"Y" or "N" Here ↑ Initial Here ↑

Place "Y" for Yes or "N" for No in the box and initial "✐" the line if the Principal desires the following:

(C) Payment Transactions

DESCRIPTION: By designating "Y" for Yes, the Agent's powers include the ability to do the following regarding **Payment Transactions**: **(01)** To pay all sums of money, at any time, which the Principal may owe in any account, bill of exchange, draft, check, purchase, contract, note, or trade acceptance made. **(02)** The ability to stop, start, execute, endorse, accept, and deliver payments by the Agent for the Principal or in the Principal name.

"Y" or "N" Here ↑ Initial Here ↑

Place "Y" for Yes or "N" for No in the box and initial "✐" the line if the Principal desires the following:

(D) Borrowing Transactions

DESCRIPTION: By designating "Y" for Yes, the Agent's powers include the ability to do the following regarding **Borrowing Transactions**: **(01)** to borrow money occasionally. **(02)** To enter, execute, renegotiate, or modify promissory notes, security deeds, or other legal agreements. **(03)** To communicate and receive information from the service lender or mortgage provider of any encumbrance, loan, or mortgage. **(04)** To pledge, encumber, or collateralize any tangible or intangible personal property except for the Principal's primary residential real estate for security purposes. **(05)** To sign, renew, extend, pay, and satisfy any notes, security instruments, or other forms of obligation from time to time, in parts or whole. The Agent borrowing capacity shall be limited to the obligations the Principal already incurred regarding existing collateral only.

"Y" or "N" Here ↑ Initial Here ↑

Place "Y" for Yes or "N" for No in the box and initial "✐" the line if the Principal desires the following:

(E) Account Receivable Transactions

DESCRIPTION: By designating "Y" for Yes, the Agent's powers include the ability to do the following regarding **Account Receivable Transactions**: **(01)** to ask for, accept, collect, receive money, receive notes payable, defer payment, dividends, interest, legacies, payment due, or property due or that may become due and owe to the Principal. **(02)** To endorse all checks or other instruments payable to the Principal and give a receipt for those payments.

"Y" or "N" Here ↑ Initial Here ↑

Place "Y" for Yes or "N" for No in the box and initial "✐" the line if the Principal desires the following:

(F) Insurance & Annuities Transactions

DESCRIPTION: By designating "Y" for Yes, the Agent's powers include the ability to do the following regarding **Insurance and Annuity Transactions**: (**01**) to procure, acquire, continue, maintain, renew, or deal with any type or combination of insurance or annuity contract. Insurance or Annuity contracts shall include (but are not limited to) life, accident, health, disability, automobile, casualty, property, and liability. (**02**) To pay premiums or assessments, surrender, and collect all distributions, proceeds, or benefits payable. The insurance or annuity contract shall stay enforced; thus, payments shall continue for the duration of this CFPOA, providing that it is economically prudent and wise. The Agent's powers do not include the ability to designate oneself as a Beneficiary of any such insurance or annuity contracts (unless their designation existed on an old policy and the Agent is trying to replace it). The Agent shall not terminate any insurance or annuity contract unless a replacement contract is active. The only exception shall occur if there is a chance to reduce insurance or annuity contract premiums with an equivalent level of insurance or annuity. The Agent shall procure insurance or annuity contracts to maximize the Principals' Wealth. If the Agent procures and acquires any insurance or annuity contract, the Beneficiary shall be one or more of the following: (**01**) a relative or Spouse of the Principal. (**02**) A trust in which a relative or Spouse of the Principal is a Beneficiary. (**03**) A Beneficiary previously designated on an insurance or annuity contract by the Principal.

"Y" or "N" Here ↑ Initial Here ↑

Place "Y" for Yes or "N" for No in the box and initial "✐" the line if the Principal desires the following:

(G) Financial Securities

DESCRIPTION: By designating "Y" for Yes, the Agent's powers include the ability to do the following regarding **Financial Securities**: (**01**) to buy, sell, exchange, surrender, assign, and redeem all types of financial securities. The financial securities shall include (but are not limited to) stocks, bonds, mutual funds, ETF, and all other investment securities and financial instruments (electronic or certificate form). (**02**) To collect, hold, and safely keep all dividends, interest, earnings, sale proceeds, distributions, shares, certificates, and other evidence of ownership paid or distributed on securities. (**03**) To transfer, sell, or exercise voting rights in connection with securities in person (at any meeting) or by proxy. (**04**) To consent, enter, modify, and limit the actions to rights associated with a voting trust. (**05**) To transfer any shares of stock, bonds, or other securities in any private or public business, corporation, association, partnership, or other legal entity for the Principal's benefit. The Agent shall not buy "on margin" or "on account" for any financial securities.

"Y" or "N" Here ↑ Initial Here ↑

Place "Y" for Yes or "N" for No in the box and initial "✐" the line if the Principal desires the following:

(H) Commodities, Futures, and Options

DESCRIPTION: By designating "Y" for Yes, the Agent's powers include the ability to do the following regarding **Commodities, Futures, and Options**: (**01**) to buy, sell, exchange, assign, convey, settle, trade, and exercise commodities, futures contracts, and put/call options on stocks and stock indices on a regulated options exchange. (**02**) The collection and receiving of revenue (proceeds or gains) deriving from commodities, futures, and option transactions. (**03**) To establish or continue commodities, futures, and option accounts for the Principal with any securities or futures broker. The Agent shall not buy "on margin" or "on account" for any financial securities; this also includes "naked call options" and "naked put options." If the Agent has no experience with commodities, futures, and option transactions or has a negative record of accomplishment, the Agent shall abstain.

"Y" or "N" Here ↑ Initial Here ↑

Place "Y" for Yes or "N" for No in the box and initial "✐" the line if the Principal desires the following:

(I) Benefits – Governmental Civilian Programs

DESCRIPTION: By designating "Y" for Yes, the Agent's powers include the ability to do the following regarding **Benefits – Governmental / Civilian Programs**: (**01**) to prepare, sign, and file any claim or application for Social Security, Unemployment, or Military Service benefits. (**02**) To sue for, settle, or abandon any claims to any benefit or assistance under any federal, state, local, or foreign statute or regulation. (**03**) To control, deposit to any account, collect, receive, take title to, and hold all benefits under any governmental or civilian program. Governmental or Civilian Programs shall include (but are not limited to) the following: Medicare, Medicaid, Social Security, Veterans, and Unemployment Benefits, and any benefits deriving from statute or regulation (local, state, federal, and foreign).

1st Witness: ______ 2nd Witness: ______ Notary Public: ______ Principal: ______

☐ "Y" or "N" Here ↑	______ Initial Here ↑	Place "Y" for Yes or "N" for No in the box and initial "✎" the line if the Principal desires the following:

(J) Tax Returns, Reports, and Transactions

DESCRIPTION: By designating "Y" for Yes, the Agent's powers include the ability to do the following regarding **Tax Returns, Reports, and Transactions**: **(01)** to prepare, make elections, sign, verify, file separate or joint income, consent to any gift, to execute and file all tax returns. **(02)** To receive and negotiate for the following: all tax refund checks, social security, unemployment insurance, governmental (reports, documents, and receipt), informational returns, and other confidential tax particulars that are required by the law (Federal, State, Local, and Foreign Government, or Taxing Authority). **(03)** To prepare, execute, and file all other papers and instruments necessary or desirable for safeguarding the Principal against illegal or excess taxation or penalties imposed for a claim's violation of any law or other governmental regulation. **(04)** To apply, pay, compromise, settle, sue, contest, object, protest, and file any claim, petition, or application concerning any audit finding, assessments, taxes, or refunds. **(05)** To deal with any taxing authorities, execute and sign on the Principal's behalf any/all Federal, State, Local, or Foreign Tax Returns (Income / Gift). Tax Return shall also include estimated returns, interest, dividends, gains, transfer, and to pay any taxes, penalties, and interest due thereon. **(06)** To allocate, apply, and initiate tax exemptions or tax clearance applications. **(07)** To make tax elections and sign any tax forms. **(07)** To receive and inspect the Principal's confidential information from any tax authority. **(08)** To receive and deposit in the Principal's bank accounts or revocable trust of the Principal the following: **(A)** checks for any refund from Federal, State, Local, and Foreign Government or Taxing Authority. **(B)** To allow the Agent to access and pay any penalties and interest incurred by the Principal by check drawn on the bank accounts or revocable trust belonging to the Principal. **(09)** To execute, offer, rescind, and restrict waivers for the Principal on tax assessment or collection of tax deficiencies and waiver of notice of disallowance of a claim for credit or refund. **(10)** To execute consents for extending or limiting the statutory period/statutes of limitations of assessing or collecting such taxes or fines. **(11)** To execute offers in compromise, offers in settlement, execution of closing agreements, and imposition of alternative taxation methods with any tax authority. **(12)** To obtain a private letter ruling on behalf of the Principal. **(13)** To receive copies of all written/electronic notices, written/electronic correspondence, and other written/electronic communications involving taxes (Local, State, Federal, or Foreign) from department personnel at an address/email of the Agent's choosing. **(14)** To receive proactive notices, updates, and communications involving taxes (Local, State, Federal, or Foreign) from department personnel. **(15)** To create, access, and transact utilizing an online business/e-business account on behalf of the Principal regarding tax matters. **Please Note:** A **Special Power of Attorney for Taxes** (**SPOAT**) is required to represent the Principal before any taxing authority (Federal, State, Local, or Foreign Government).

☐ "Y" or "N" Here ↑	______ Initial Here ↑	Place "Y" for Yes or "N" for No in the box and initial "✎" the line if the Principal desires the following:

(K) Legal – Litigation, Claims and Disputes

DESCRIPTION: By designating "Y" for Yes, the Agent's powers include the ability to do the following regarding **Legal – Litigation, Claims, and Disputes**: **(01)** to commence/engage in any of the following: administrative proceedings, legal proceedings, or lawsuits. That may be in connection with any matter currently pending or may occur in the future between the Principal and any person, firm, corporation, or other legal entity. **(02)** To prosecute, appeal, answer, appear, defend, demand, discontinue, abandon, compound, compromise, arbitrate, maintain, make allowance, settle, adjust, and dispose of any claim or litigation for or against the Principal or Principal's property. **(03)** To collect and receive any claim or settlement proceeds. **(04)** To waive or release any rights belonging to the Principal. **(05)** To employ attorneys, representatives, et cetera, and sign legitimate legal contracts, contingency agreements, et cetera as deemed necessary and prudent concerning such litigation.

BEWARE:	THE FOLLOWING POWER, IF ACTIVATED, GIVES THE AGENT THE AUTHORITY TO EMPLOY OTHER INDIVIDUALS.

☐ "Y" or "N" Here ↑	______ Initial Here ↑	Place "Y" for Yes or "N" for No in the box and initial "✎" the line if the Principal desires the following:

(L) Hiring Representatives

DESCRIPTION: By designating "Y" for Yes, the Agent's powers include the ability to do the following regarding **Hiring Representatives**: **(01)** to hire or employ the following: accountants, attorneys, consultants, clerks, physicians, nurses, servants, workers, and other personnel that are prudent and proper. **(02)** To employ, hire, fire, appoint other individuals in their stead, and pay salaries, wages, or other remuneration as the Agent shall deem proper, prudent, and fair.

Place "Y" for Yes or "N" for No in the box and initial "✐" the line if the Principal desires the following:

(M) Estate, Trust, and other Beneficiary Transactions

"Y" or "N" Here ↑ Initial Here ↑

DESCRIPTION: By designating "Y" for Yes, the Agent's powers include the ability to do the following regarding **Estate, Trust, and other Beneficiary Transactions**: (**01**) to accept, receive, exercise, release, reject, renounce, assign, disclaim, demand, and sue. (**02**) To recover any inheritance, legacy, bequest, devise, gift, or other property interests of the Principal. (**03**) To assert any interest in and exercise power over any trust, estate, or property subject to fiduciary control. (**04**) To establish a revocable trust (for the Principal's benefit) that terminates upon death; afterward, it shall be the Executor/Administrator of the Principal's estate responsibility. The Agent shall not amend, change, create, or revoke a last will or revocable trust that the Principal made. The Agent shall not require or force the Trustee of any trust to pay income to the Principal's Agent unless a specific authority allows such transactions. Any financial assets, income, or property received by the Principal, in part or whole, by the following methods: (**A**) Inheritance by operation of law (joint tenancy with the right of survivorship, last will). (**B**) Benefits (monetary assets) are defined by the operation of contract law to a beneficiary (insurance or annuity policy, IRA, pension plan, investment, or financial account). The Principal directs that the Agent shall transfer any/all interest that the Principal may have in the property, whether real or personal, intangible or tangible, to the Trustee of any trust that the Principal creates or for the Principal's benefit if appropriate and prudent. In the unlikely event that the Principal's health condition results in the following: (**01**) have a disability that renders the Principal functioning non-socially. (**02**) The Principal is incapacitated. (**03**) The Principal is incompetent. Upon diagnosis, the Agent shall have the power to terminate or direct the administration of any trust that the Principal is a Beneficiary. The Agent may act only if these (**03**) three criteria are present. (**01**) It is prudent, wise, and reasonable. (**02**) The Agent has written consent from at least two-thirds of the Trustees (active and inactive). (**03**) The Agent establishes and files a realistic plan of action either with the Trustee(s) or with the court(s). At least two-thirds of the Trustee(s) must agree with the Agent's proposed plan regarding the Trust Assets, or the Judge must approve the plan regarding the Trust Assets.

Place "Y" for Yes or "N" for No in the box and initial "✐" the line if the Principal desires the following:

(N) Retirement Plan or Benefits Transactions

"Y" or "N" Here ↑ Initial Here ↑

DESCRIPTION: By designating "Y" for Yes, the Agent's powers include the ability to do the following regarding **Retirement Plan or Benefit Transactions**: (**01**) to contribute, transfer assets between, withdraw, and deposit funds in any retirement plan. Retirement plans shall include (but are not limited to) any pension, profit-sharing, stock bonus, employee savings or equivalent plan, individual retirement account (IRA), deferred compensation plan, and any other type of employee benefit plan. (**02**) To make rollover contributions from any retirement plan to other retirement plans or individual retirement accounts; exercise all investment powers available under any self-directed retirement plan. (**03**) To make, select, and change payment options (timing, method, withdrawals amount, distribution, and rollovers), calculate minimum required distributions and methods of distribution as a beneficiary of a qualified retirement plan or an IRA. The Agent shall not transfer any assets in a retirement plan that will be financially detrimental to the Principal or any of the Principal's beneficiaries.

Place "Y" for Yes or "N" for No in the box and initial "✐" the line if the Principal desires the following:

(O) Other Terms: (Conditions, Prohibitions, Restriction, Exceptions, Additions, Limitation, Extensions, and Special Rules)

"Y" or "N" Here ↑ Initial Here ↑

DESCRIPTION: By designating "Y" for Yes, the Agent's powers may be subject to the following regarding **Other Terms**: conditions, prohibitions, restrictions, exceptions, additions, limitations, extensions, or any special rules as typed in the box below. If there are any contradictions concerning **Article IX Subsections A through N,** the Principal shall type a brief explanation for the contradiction.

Specify in Detail

Preferably Type or Legible writing in Ink

Article X: Restrictions on Agent's Powers

Regardless of what authorization or powers bestow in **Article IX Subsection A through N,** the Agent shall not do or perform the following: **(01)** The Agent shall not make a loan to oneself, another name Agent, or a beneficiary of the Agent. **(02)** The Agent shall not take a service fee as an Agent. **(03)** The Agent shall not create, modify, or revoke a trust. **(04)** The Agent shall not use the Principal's property to fund a trust for someone other than the Principal or a trust that does not benefit the Principal greater than seventy (70%) percent. **(05)** The Agent shall not create or change a Beneficiary's interest in the Principal's property. **(06)** The Agent shall not create or change the Principal's interest in the Principal's property solely for the benefit of another. **(07)** The Agent shall not designate or change the designation of beneficiaries to receive any property, benefit, or contract right on the Principal's death. **(08)** The Agent shall not make or revoke a gift of the Principal property in trust or another arrangement. **(09)** The Agent shall not make or revoke a gift on the Principal's behalf. **(10)** The Agent shall not exercise any powers that would cause the Principal's assets to become taxable to the Agent or the Agent's estate for any income, estate, or inheritance tax. **(11)** The Agent shall not forgive debts owed to the Principal, disclaim, or waive benefits payable to the Principal. **(12)** The Agent shall not execute, publish, declare, amend, or revoke the following: last will, codicil, or any will substitute on the Principal's behalf. **(13)** The Agent shall not perform duties under a contract that requires the Principal's services. **(14)** The Agent shall not make an affidavit about the Principal's knowledge that is unknown to the Agent personally. **(15)** The Agent shall not vote in any governmental public election on behalf of the Principal unless the Agent has a notarized letter stating who the Principal's candidates and voting preferences are regarding that public election. **(16)** The Agent shall not exercise powers and authority granted to the Principal as Trustee or a court-appointed Fiduciary. **(17)** The Agent shall not exercise the right to make a disclaimer on behalf of the Principal, except for a disclaimer of a detrimental transfer or acceptance made with the court's approval. **(18)** The Agent shall not enjoin (add or transfer) ownership or title to the Principal´s funds or assets in the Agent's name alone. **Please Note:** Waiver of these restrictions shall only occur if the Principal grants written permission in **Article IX Subsection O**.

1st Witness: ______ 2nd Witness: ______ Notary Public: ______ Principal: ______

Article XI: Revocation

A: The Principal may revoke the CFPOA in writing for any reason without prior notice to the Agent or any Third Parties. However, in part(s) or whole, any Revocation shall require a Notary Public attesting to the revocation to ensure the authenticity and legitimacy of the Principal's actions.

B: Revocation Methods: Revocation of this CFPOA shall only occur in part(s) or whole by the following methods: (**01**) A new CFPOA that states all prior CFPOAs are revoked in writing. (**02**) The Principal revokes the CFPOA in a formal (type) manner with the Principal's signature and notarization. (**03**) The Principal willfully destroys all original (sign and seal) CFPOA and requests the destruction of all copies in writing. (**04**) The appropriate authorities have declared the death of the Principal. (**05**) A court of competent jurisdiction has issued a court order to terminate the Principal's CFPOA, in parts or whole.

C: All other Revocation methods shall be invalid and unenforceable, even if they are legally allowable.

Article XII: Protector

SAFETY FEATURE: Implementing this option creates an administrative burden, but it also creates checks and balances. This option is a personal decision that the Principal must make for their future benefit.

[ ] "Y" or "N" Here ↑ ______ Initial Here ↑

Place "Y" for Yes or "N" for No in the box and initial "✐" the line if the Principal desires the following:

Restrict Agent's Powers by using a Protector

By designating "Y" for Yes, the Principal has enacted a Durable Protecting Power of Attorney (DPPOA). The role of the Protector is to safeguard the best interest and wishes of the Principal, primarily in a passive capacity, and to provide basic administrative support to the Agent. However, when the Agent violates their role as a Fiduciary, it is the role of the Protector to step in, relieve the Agent, and protect the Principal's rights and interests.

The date of DPPOA Execution: **Month of:** ______ **Day of:** ______ **Year of:** ______

A formal recording/filing (optional) of the DPPOA is with the following:

Public Records:			
Location:		**Docket #**	
Address:		**Page #**	

The Principal designates the Protector (the first choice) with decision-making powers to adhere to the terms within the DPPOA.

Protector 1st choice →				
Full Name:				
Address:				
Phone #:		**Email:**		
Residence:	**County:**		**State:**	

In the unlikely event that the Protector (the first choice) refuses, is unable, or is denied (by a Judge or Principal) to act as a Protector. The Principal designates the successor Protector (the second choice) with decision-making powers to adhere to the terms within the DPPOA.

Protector 2nd choice →				
Full Name:				
Address:				
Phone #:		**Email:**		
Residence:	**County:**		**State:**	

In the unlikely event that the Protector (the second choice) refuses, is unable, or is denied (by a Judge or Principal) to act as a Protector. The Principal dictates that a court of legal jurisdiction shall appoint a Protector for the Principal with decision-making powers to adhere to the terms within the DPPOA.

A: An active Protector shall not serve as an acting Agent; this is to prevent a conflict of interest. The individual must either abstain or resign from one of the roles to perform the functions of the other.

B: The Protector (listed above) must be an Agent within the DPPOA to have power over the CFPOA's Agents. The choice selection for Protector may not be in the same order as shown on the CFPOA; if there is a conflict regarding choice selection designation, the CFPOA shall take precedence.

Article XIII: Durability Provisions

Statement of Understanding by the Principal: The Principal understands that the direction and choices implemented by the Agent as specified in this CFPOA (if still active due to durability provision(s) and not previously revoked) shall continue, even if the Principal objects to the actions or decisions later when the Principal is functioning non-socially, incapacitated, or incompetent.

DIRECTIONS: The Principal must **place "Y"** for **Yes** in all applicable empty box spaces below and initial "✎" on **the line** for activation of Durable Power(s). The Principal must **place "N"** for **No** to all applicable empty box spaces below **and initial "✎" the line** for no activation of Durable Power(s). Durable Power(s) will not receive activation if the empty box space or the Principal's initial is void or left blank.

[ ] "Y" or "N" Here ↑ ______ Initial Here ↑

Place "Y" for Yes or "N" for No in the box and initial "✎" the line if the Principal desires the following:

(A) Durability against Incompetence

DESCRIPTION: By designating "Y" for Yes, this CFPOA shall continue if the Principal becomes incompetent; this CFPOA shall survive the effects of incompetence and shall not be invalid, null, or void. Furthermore, the Agent's power and authority shall remain effective when the Principal is incompetent.

[ ] "Y" or "N" Here ↑ ______ Initial Here ↑

Place "Y" for Yes or "N" for No in the box and initial "✎" the line if the Principal desires the following:

(B) Durability against Incapacity

DESCRIPTION: By designating "Y" for Yes, this CFPOA shall continue if the Principal becomes incapacitated; this CFPOA shall survive the effects of incapacity and shall not be invalid, null, or void. Furthermore, the Agent's power and authority shall remain effective when the Principal is incapacitated.

[ ] "Y" or "N" Here ↑ ______ Initial Here ↑

Place "Y" for Yes or "N" for No in the box and initial "✎" the line if the Principal desires the following:

(C) Durability against Functioning Non-Socially

DESCRIPTION: By designating "Y" for Yes, this CFPOA shall continue if the Principal functions Non-Socially; this CFPOA shall survive the effects of functioning non-socially and shall not be invalid, null, or void. Furthermore, the Agent's power and authority shall remain effective when the Principal functions non-socially.

Recommendation:	The Agent should attach the **Affidavit of Principal's Health State** by a licensed Health Professional (dated before the expiration date) if the Principal is functioning non-socially, incapacitated, or incompetent when presenting the CFPOA to any Third Party.

Article XIV: Additional Legal Provisions

A: Reliance by Third Parties: To induce any Third Party to act, the Principal agrees that any Third Party receiving a duly executed copy/facsimile of this CFPOA may act upon hereunder. The revocation shall be ineffective until the Third Party receives notice or knowledge of the revocation. The Principal, Principal's heir(s), executor(s), administrator(s), legal or personal representative(s), and assign(s) agree to indemnify and hold harmless to the Third Party from and against all claims due to relying upon this CFPOA.

B: Notice to Third Party: A Third Party who fails to honor a properly executed CFPOA may be liable to the Principal, the Agent, the Principal's heirs, assigns, or estate. Liabilities may include (but are not limited to) the following: civil penalty plus damages, costs, and fees associated with the failure to comply with the CFPOA.

C: Compensation: Any individual serving in a fiduciary capacity in adherence to this CFPOA shall not receive compensation for the performance of their authority, rights, and responsibilities. However, the Fiduciary may receive reimbursement (if possible) for reasonable and necessary expenses incurred in performing their authority, rights, and responsibilities. If the Principal wishes to compensate the Agent, the Principal shall specify in detail in **Article IX Subsection O**.

D: Binding on Successors: This CFPOA and all its provisions shall become effective upon execution. All provisions shall be binding upon the heir(s), executor(s), administrator(s), legal or personal representative(s), and assign(s) and all fiduciaries' successors of the Principal as fully allowable by law.

1st Witness: ______ **2nd Witness:** ______ **Notary Public:** ______ **Principal:** ______

E: Original Counterparts: If multiple originals of this CFPOA have been executed, each such counterpart original shall have equal force and effect. Any photocopy of this CFPOA shall have the same force and effect as the original. **Suggestion:** Shade the Notary Public Seal when making a photocopy of CFPOA.

F: Surety or Bond: No individual named as an approved Agent selected for consideration by a Judge shall require the filing or furnishing of a bond, surety, or other security in any jurisdiction. If, despite this CFPOA, a bond is necessary, the Principal requests that it be without sureties and in a nominal amount.

G: Indemnification of Fiduciary: No individual serving within a fiduciary capacity named in this CFPOA shall incur any liability by the Principal for acting or refraining from acting under this CFPOA except in instances of the Fiduciary's negligence or wanton, willful, or reckless misconduct.

H: Indemnification of Third Parties: Third Parties that act in good faith, based on this CFPOA, shall not be subject to liability (criminal or civil) or professional disciplinary action for such reliance, except for the Third Parties' negligence or wanton, willful, or reckless misconduct.

I: Recordation: Recording this CFPOA with the county auditor, recording officer, et cetera is permissible, provided it serves a practical legal purpose or reason.

J: Relative Conflict: If the approved Agent selected for consideration by a Judge is a Spouse or is an Adult Child/Ward of the Principal. The Principal waives any conflict of interest that their Spouse or Adult Child/Ward might have due to potential inheritance or beneficiary arrangements.

K: Definition of Child/Ward: As used in this CFPOA, "Child" shall include any individual the Principal legally adopts. The term "Ward" shall consist of any individual legally in the Principal's care who is also the acting Guardian.

L: Fiduciaries: The term Fiduciaries shall include the following: Agent, Medical Health Care Surrogate, Mental Health Care Surrogate, Guardian, or Conservator. Be aware that the Principal reserves the right to designate or nominate other individuals as Fiduciaries in other legal documents to act on the Principal's behalf.

M: Transfer of Fiduciary Powers: No Agent shall have the rights or powers to any acts, power, duty, right, or obligation relating to any person, matter, transaction, or property in which the Principal is serving as a Fiduciary (Trustee, custodian, or personal representative) for someone else.

N: Modification: Upon execution, changes to this CFPOA shall not occur. If the Principal wants to change this CFPOA, the Principal must make an entirely new one. However, revocation of any part(s) of this CFPOA may occur if it is in writing; once a part(s) receives revocation, it shall be permanent. Alterations (strikes out, cross out, and blackouts) of any provisions or writing within this CFPOA shall have no bearing in a court of law and shall remain active and valid as to their original intent.

O: Picture I.D.: The Principal requires verifying the Agent's identity with a government-issued picture ID. The Principal does not require it to be current and up to date; all that the Principal requires is the ability to confirm their facial features in a picture from an official governmental source.

P: Delegation: The Agent shall not delegate their power or rights to individuals unless **Article XVII** (**Authorization of Delegation of Agent's Power to another Agent**) is active.

Q: Durability: If one or more of the durability provisions in **Article XIII** is active and applicable, then this CFPOA shall remain viable and legally enforceable unless the Principal, while in a Healthy State, implements a Revocation in adherence to **Article XI Subsection B.**

R: Conflicting Provisions: If one or more provisions conflict due to the scope and nature of the powers given, the Fiduciary powers shall be reduced in the provision or a subset thereof that is more conservative and prudent in scope and nature.

S: Headings (Article & Subsection): Article and Subsection Headings in Bold Face are for informational purposes only and serve as a guide to what the subject entails. However, the heading may not be all-inclusive or reflect all the information about that article, provision, or description. Thus, it behooves the Principal, Agent, and all Third Parties to read the article, provision, or description carefully and with due diligence.

T: Governing Law: This CFPOA shall take effect immediately as a sealed instrument and shall receive interpretation, enforcement, and governance under the State's laws where the Principal has established physical residency at the time of enforcement. The Principal requests for the honoring of this CFPOA in any State, County, or Location in which the Principal's body or property may be, with the intention that it be valid in all jurisdictions/territories of the United States and all Foreign Nations. This CFPOA is to receive the most liberal interpretation available to grant the appointed Fiduciary the greatest amount of decision-making discretion.

1st Witness: _______ 2nd Witness: _______ Notary Public: _______ Principal: _______

U: Severability / Saving Clause: An invalid or unenforceable provision within this CFPOA might exist. If that occurs, the remaining provisions of this CFPOA shall continue and be active as if said invalid or unenforceable provision did not exist. All remaining provisions shall be undisturbed to maintain their original legal meaning, force, and effect. If a court finds or deems that an invalidated or unenforceable provision will become valid if limitations exist, then such written provision shall receive a written modification by court order to limit the provision's power while maximizing the economic value and liberties granted.

V: Lapse of Time: A lapse of time shall not affect the validity or effectiveness of this CFPOA.

W: Legal Document Priority: If a court of competent jurisdiction appoints a Guardian or Conservator to oversee and manage the Principal's property, the Principal intended that this CFPOA take precedence over all other means of ascertaining the Principal's intentions. The Principal intends that this CFPOA shall not endure subjugation or subterfuge by any acting Guardian or Conservator unless the area in question is ambiguous. The Guardian or Conservator shall have wide latitude and discretion in their duties in ambiguous cases.

X: Court Appointed Guardian or Conservator: the Principal intends by this CFPOA to avoid a court-supervised guardianship or conservatorship. If the Principal attempts or fails to avoid a court-supervised guardianship or conservatorship. Then, the Principal requests that the Agent designated in this CFPOA serve as Guardian or Conservator of the Principal's property and affairs. The court-appointed Guardian or Conservator shall not have the power to revoke, suspend, or terminate this CFPOA or the Agent's powers except as specifically authorized by law. The Principal may execute the following: "**Declaration of Guardianship & Conservatorship**," if execution occurs, the Principal prefers that those individuals act in such a fiduciary capacity.

Y: Specific Forms or In-House POA: If a Third Party refuses to recognize this CFPOA and requires a specific form or in-house Power of Attorney. The Agent can execute said legal document immediately subject to the limitations and rights established in this CFPOA with a permanent attachment of this CFPOA to said document.

Article XV: Acknowledgment by the Agent

A: The Agent shall exercise due care and act in the Principal's best interest with the powers granted while adhering to any limitations, impositions, or specifications within this CFPOA.

B: The Agent's foremost duty is loyalty and protection of the Principal and the Principal's interests. The Agent shall direct any benefits derived from this CFPOA to the Principal. The Agent must avoid conflicts of interest and use ordinary skill and prudence to exercise these powers. If there is anything about this CFPOA or the Agent's duties that the Agent does not understand, the Agent shall seek professional advice.

C: A court of competent jurisdiction has the discretion to revoke the Agent's power, especially if acting inappropriately. Thus, it behooves the Agent to exercise the bestowed powers in a fiduciary manner. The burden will be upon the Agent to prove that such acts were prudent and within a Fiduciary standard for any questionable acts. The Agent may be liable for damages and subject to criminal and civil prosecution if a court of competent jurisdiction finds that the Agent has violated their fiduciary duty.

D: The Agent has the power to abstain from using their granted powers under this CFPOA; however, the Agent does not have the luxury of being negligent when the **Life, Safety**, and **Welfare** of the Principal are at stake. The Agent may be liable for damages, be subject to prosecution (criminal or civil), and suffer termination of powers if a court rules that the Agent has been negligent regarding their fiduciary duty under this CFPOA to the Principal,

E: The Agent agrees to keep all monetary funds or financial assets that belong to the Principal in separate accounts from the Agent's monetary funds or financial assets. There shall be no commingling of monetary funds or financial assets to ensure simple accounting and safeguard the Principal's financial security. Furthermore, the Agent agrees to protect, conserve, and exercise prudence and caution in dealings with the Principal's monetary funds, financial assets, and all other assets of value and worth.

F: The Agent agrees to keep a complete/accurate record of all acts, disbursements, and receipts for review/inspection. The Agent agrees to provide an accounting/report to the Principal or Protector at the following time intervals (as stated below). If the Principal dies, the Executor/Administrator of the Principal's estate shall receive the accounting/report within a quarter. **Directions: Place a "✓" in the Accounting / Report Period box.**

Report Period: ☐ **None** ☐ **Monthly** ☐ **Quarterly** ☐ **Annually**

G: By default, the Agent shall not receive compensation for their authority, rights, and responsibilities; however, the Agent may receive reimbursement for reasonable and necessary expenses incurred in performing their authority, rights, and responsibilities. The Principal may compensate the Agent if the Principal desires.

H: The Agent shall disclose all actions that require written authorization by using their identity as the Agent in the following manner: (Agent's Signature) as Agent for (Principal's Name).

I: For Simple and Special POA, the Agent may resign by notifying the Principal or the Principal's Guardian or Conservator (provided a Judge appoints one). For Complex and Durable POA, the Agent may resign by notifying the Principal, Protector, Co-Agent, Successor Agent, or the Principal's Guardian or Conservator (provided a Judge appoints one). The resignation must be in writing and sent by certified mail, statutory overnight delivery (return receipt requested), or email.

J: If the Agent becomes aware of the death of the Principal who executed the CFPOA, the Agent must notify all Third Parties as soon as practicable that the Principal has died and that this CFPOA is no longer legitimate and effective. If Durability Provision(s) are not active or applicable, the Agent must notify all Third Parties as soon as practicable that the Principal is functioning non-socially, incapacitated, or incompetent; thus, the CFPOA is no longer valid.

K: If the Agent resigns or ceases to represent the Principal regarding this CFPOA, the former Agent agrees to return all property and documents to the Principal or the Protector (if **Article XII** is active).

L: The Agent agrees to keep all information (financial, relationship, or other personal matters) confidential and shall not disclose it to any outsiders unless those individuals are relevant Third Parties that require such information.

M: The Agent is responsible for informing the Principal of changes in their physical address or contact information.

N: If the Durable Provision(s) is active, the Agent may need to sign an Affidavit that the CFPOA is in Full Force and Effect to induce any Third Party to act.

O: The Agent understands that their power and rights are limited and shall be subservient to the Protector if **Article XII** is active. Upon request, the Principal or Protector shall provide the Agent with a copy of the Durable Protecting Power of Attorney, preferably by email as a PDF attachment.

P: If **Article XVI** is active, all Agents agree to implement the **Acknowledgment of Appointment by Agent** and proactively mail a copy to the Principal or Protector (if applicable).

Q: If **Article XVI** is active, all Agents wishing to resign shall fill out and sign the **Acknowledgment of Resignation by Agent** and proactively mail the original notarized Acknowledgment of Resignation by Agent to the Principal or Protector (if applicable).

R: The Agent accepts this appointment subserviently to CFPOA's terms and conditions. The Agent agrees to act and perform reasonably and prudently in a fiduciary capacity with the Principal's best interests in mind. However, the powers granted to the Agent shall expire upon the Principal death. If Durability Provision(s) are not active or applicable, the powers granted to the Agent shall automatically expire if the Principal is functioning non-socially, incapacitated, or incompetent.

Article XVI: Acknowledgment of Appointment by the Agent

SAFETY FEATURE: Implementing this option creates an administrative burden, but it also creates checks and balances. This option is a personal decision that the Principal must make for their future benefit.

[ ] "Y" or "N" Here ↑ ______ Initial Here ↑

Place "Y" for Yes or "N" for No in the box and initial "✎" the line if the Principal desires the following:

Requires Utilization of Acknowledgment of Appointment by Agent Form

For brevity and consistency, the abbreviation of "**Acknowledgment of Appointment by Agent**" shall be "**Appointment.**" By designating "Y" for Yes, the Principal requires the Agent to fill out, sign, and notarize the Appointment as a condition of becoming the acting Agent. The Agent shall forfeit their right to serve as an Agent by default if the Agent fails to implement the Appointment. The successor Agent shall become the current acting Agent, provided the successor Agent executes the Appointment. The appointment shall become a prerequisite for the Agent to implement in all succession matters. If the Principal selects a Co-Power Sharing for Agents, implementing this Appointment shall still be a requirement for each Agent. When utilizing the CFPOA with any Third Party, the Agent shall provide a copy of the Appointment to the Third Party. Failure to provide a copy of the Appointment to the Third Party shall result in the Third Party refusing and declining the CFPOA.

1st Witness: ______ 2nd Witness: ______ Notary Public: ______ Principal: ______

Article XVII: Authorization of Delegation of Agent's Power to another Agent

SAFETY FEATURE: Implementing this option creates an administrative burden, but it also creates checks and balances. This option is a personal decision that the Principal must make for their future benefit.

[ ] "Y" or "N" Here ↑ ______ Initial Here ↑

Place "Y" for Yes or "N" for No in the box and initial "✎" the line if the Principal desires the following:

Delegation of Agent's Powers to another Agent

By designating "Y" for Yes, the Principal allows delegating an Agent's powers to another Agent in **Article VII**. This discretionary power is useful when the acting Agent suffers inconveniences due to a lack of knowledge, logistics issues, or time constraints. The Agent who receives power from another Agent is the "Delegate." For transparency and record-keeping purposes, the utilization of the following forms shall occur: "**Delegation of Agent's Powers**" and "**Revocation of Delegate by (Agent, Principal, or Protector)**" with a copy mailed by the Agent to the Principal. If the Principal revokes an Agent, and the Agent has a Delegate, then the Delegate's powers are no longer active. If the Principal or Protector revokes an Agent due to a violation of Fiduciary duties, then that Agent shall not serve in the future as a Delegate. If the Principal or Protector revokes a Delegate for violating Fiduciary duties, then that Delegate shall not serve as an Agent forever.

Article XVIII: Security Footer Setting

SAFETY FEATURE: To prevent fraud and ensure legitimacy, the Principal may desire to enact a security feature known as the "**Security Footer**." Security Footer is burdensome; however, if the Principal believes that a party will contest or illegitimately alter this CFPOA, selecting the "High" setting may be desirable. The following pages will not usually have a security feature: (**01**) Cover Page, (**02**) Table of Contents, (**03**) Warning Page, (**04**) Informational Page, and (**05**) Intentionally blank separate page. The Principal requires the CFPOA to have the following security setting: **Directions: Place a "✓" in the Security Level box.**

Security Level: [ ] **None** [ ] **Low** [ ] **Moderate** [ ] **High**

If the security selection is "**None**," no initial on the Security Footer is required. If the security selection is "**Low**," then the Principal's initial is required in the Security Footer. If the security selection is "**Moderate**," then the Principal's and Notary's initials are required in the Security Footer. If the security selection is "**High**," then the Principal's, Notary's, and Witness's initial is required in the Security Footer. The default option is "None" if the security selection is left blank (not "✓").

A: It might be suspicious if a page within this CFPOA lacks the necessary initials, as stated in the Security Footer setting indicated above. In this event, the whole page shall be invalid and deemed unenforceable.

B: If a Witness but not the other Witness (when (**02**) two Witnesses are required) forgot to initial the Security Footer, but the Notary and Principal initial that page, then that page shall survive **Article XVIII, Subsection A**. However, if no Notary's initial is present in the Security Footer and the Witness's initial is missing, then that page shall be subject to **Article XVIII, Subsection A.**

C: Under State Law, if this CFPOA is valid and enforceable with a Security Footer level of "Moderate," even though it is supposed to have a "High" Security Footer level." Then the following shall apply: If one or both Witnesses do not initial the Security Footer even though the Security Footer level is "High," then that page shall survive **Article XVIII, Subsection A**, providing that the Principal and Notary have initialed the page.

D: If the Security Footer requires a Notary's Initial and the Notary's Initial is not present, the page shall be subject to **Article XVIII, Subsection A.**

E: If the Security Footer requires a Principal's Initial and the Principal's Initial is not present, the page shall be subject to **Article XVIII, Subsection A.**

F: If a Witness is also a potential Health Care Surrogate, Mental Health Care Surrogate, Agent, Guardian, or Conservator, then due to conflict of interest, the Witness shall not serve in such a fiduciary capacity unless the Witness gets approval through a court of competent jurisdiction to act in a fiduciary role.

G: To prevent fraud, every revocation requires a Notary Initial, Signature, and Seal; one or more Witnesses are not required.

Article XIX: Ambiguities Interpretation Instructions

A: If a provision requires that a specific section be "Type" to be valid, failure to **"Type"** the section shall make that part invalid, null, and void.

B: If a provision requires that a specific section have the **Principal's Initial** for it to be valid, failure to initial the section shall make that part invalid, null, and void.

C: If a fillable section is **blank**, thus not typed or filled in, the legal interpretation shall be that the Principal did not intend for that section to be effective, and when it comes to interpreting that section, it shall be invalid, null, and void.

D: If a fillable section requires a **Yes "Y"** or **No "N"** and the section is blank (thus not typed or filled in), the legal interpretation shall be that the Principal did not intend for that section to be effective; therefore, it shall be **No** "N."

E: If a fillable section requires a **Yes "Y"** or **No "N;"** however, **"Yes"** or **"No"** exists instead, the legal interpretation shall be that the Principal did intend for that section to keep its legal effect and meaning.

F: If a fillable section requires a **Check "✓"** and it is blank, thus not typed or filled in, the legal interpretation shall be that the Principal did not intend for that section to be effective; therefore, not wanted.

G: If a fillable section gives multiple options that are mutually exclusive to each other in which a **Check "✓"** is required if more than one option is checked "✓" then the legal interpretation shall be that the Principal did this in error; thus when it comes to interpreting that section, the implementation shall be of the more conservative option.

H: If a fillable section requires a **Check "✓"** or "X," however a dash "—" exists instead, the legal interpretation shall be that the Principal did not intend for that section to be effective; thus, it is not wanted.

I: If a section or provision is typed with added handwritten instructions, only the "typed" section will receive consideration concerning the Principal's intentions. The rationale is simple: any person, not necessarily the Principal, can handwrite (ink in) after the fact. Due to a lack of verification, the additional handwritten instruction shall be invalid, null, and void.

J: Most state laws will void a legal document if someone writes on the surface, especially after notarization or execution. The Principal waives this right since the formalization of the CFPOA requires it to be typed and printed; thus, any handwritten alteration concerning the altered section shall be unsubstantial and nonbearing unless an unaltered original duplicate or legitimate copy is available; only the unreadable section shall be invalid, null, and void.

K: If this CFPOA allows handwritten statements by the Principal and there seem to be any suspicious alterations or additions (changes in handwriting style, changes in ink), such handwritten alterations or additions shall have no weight or bearing. Unless an unaltered original duplicate or legitimate copy is available, the altered section shall only be invalid, null, and void if it (the altered section) is unreadable as to its original intentions.

L: The Descriptions that follow a **Yes** "Y" or a **No** "N" Box are for clarification and informational purposes to outline the performance of duties and rights.

M: If a Third Party receives more than one active Power of Attorney regarding the Principal: (**01**) The Power of Attorney that has the most recent date shall take more precedence unless otherwise stated in **Article IX Subsection O**. (**02**) If the Principal function non-socially, incapacitated, or incompetent, then the Power of Attorney that has an active Durability Provision(s), in effect, shall take precedence. (**03**) If the Power of Attorney has the same date, then a General Power takes precedence over a Financial Power of Attorney. A Financial Power of Attorney takes precedence over a Banking Power of Attorney. A Limited Power of Attorney shall be subservient to a General, Financial, and Banking Power of Attorney if any conflicts arise. (**04**) A Protecting Power of Attorney shall stand alone and only be binding upon Complex and Durable Power of Attorney with active Protector provisions. (**05**) A Complex Power of Attorney takes precedence over a Simple Power of Attorney if any conflicts arise. (**06**) Unless otherwise specified within a Special Power of Attorney, a Special Power of Attorney shall take precedence over a Complex and Simple Power of Attorney if there are any conflicts.

Article XX: Signature and Execution

In the presence of (**02**) two Witnesses and a Notary, the Principal has executed this CFPOA. The Principal understands the full import and meaning of this CFPOA and is aware that this CFPOA gives the Agent **the powers to handle financial activities and perform financial transactions**. The Principal reaffirms the following in the Witnesses and Notary presence: (**01**) The Principal is at least eighteen (**18**) years or older. (**02**) The Principal is of sound and disposing mind (emotionally and mentally competent) to make or request this CFPOA. (**03**) The Principal has the capacity with full memory or necessary mental faculties to understand and comprehend these actions. (**04**) The Principal willfully and voluntarily executes this CFPOA. (**05**) The Principal declares under the Penalty of Perjury that this paragraph is true and correct.

Principal →	**Full Legal Name:**		**Signature:**	**Thumb/Finger Print:**
	Today's Date:			**Real Estate Transaction**

Have (02) two Adult Witness* the Principal's signature in addition to having their signature notarized*

In the joint presence of each other, the Witnesses State that the Principal is the following: (**01**) The Principal is at least eighteen (**18**) years or older. (**02**) The Principal is of sound and disposing mind (emotionally and mentally competent). (**03**) The Principal is not suffering from constraint, duress, fraud, or undue influence. (**04**) The Principal acknowledges having willfully and voluntarily dated and signed this CFPOA (or asked/directed for such actions to occur). (**05**) The Witnesses affirm that they have no direct biological or marital relationship with the Principal and are not a Beneficiary of the Principal's estate. (**06**) The Witnesses affirm their impartiality and confirm that the criterion stated in the box at the bottom of the last page does not apply. (**07**) The Witnesses declare this paragraph true and correct under the Penalty of Perjury.

If the Witness is uncomfortable giving out personal contact information, current employment information and occupation will suffice.

1st Witness →	**Name:**		**Signature:**	
	Address:			
	Phone #:		**Date:**	
	Occupation:			

2nd Witness Or Special Witness ** →	**Name:**		**Signature:**	
	Address:			
	Phone #:		**Date:**	
	Occupation:			

UNDER THE LAWS OF → COUNTY: ______________________

STATE: ______________________

Before the Notary Public (the undersigned authority) comes forth, the Principal, with a sound/disposed mind, is eighteen (**18**) years or older. The Principal acknowledges having willfully and voluntarily dated and signed this CFPOA (or asked/directed for such actions to occur) stated above in the Notary Public presence. If Witnesses sign and attest that the Principal has signed this CFPOA, the Notary Public shall attest that the Witnesses have signed this CFPOA in the Notary Public's presence. Furthermore, the Notary Public states that the Principal has provided a Government Issue identification card with a facial picture to prove identity. The Notary Public declares under the Penalty of Perjury that this paragraph is true and correct.

If the Principal or Witnesses sign this CFPOA but not in the presence of the Notary Public, then the Notary Public will not notarize or sign this CFPOA.

* Notary Public →				
	Full Name:		**Signature & Seal:**	
	Location:			
	Address:			
	Phone #:		**I.D. Number:**	
	Date:		**Commission Expires:**	

*** None shall serve as a Witness, Notary Public, or other qualified individual with the authority to administer oaths regarding this CFPOA made under this section.**

(**01**) Any individual related to the Principal by blood, marriage, or adoption. (**02**) Any individual currently a Beneficiary of the Principal's estate (laws of intestate succession or any existing will/codicil). (**03**) Any individual who benefits from a financial policy (insurance or annuity) in which the Principal's life is insured. (**04**) Any individual claiming (present/inchoate) any part of the Principal's estate. (**05**) Any individual who serves as an Owner, Operator, or employee of a Health Care Facility (Medical, Mental, or Assisted Living) in which the Principal is currently a Patient / Client unless the employee serves solely as a Notary Public. (**06**) Any Doctor, Physician, Psychologist, Psychiatrist, Social Worker, Financial Advisor, or Financial Manager in which the Principal is currently a Patient / Client. (**07**) Any individual who serves as an Owner, Operator, or employee of a Final Dispositional Facility (Funerary Home, Crematory Authority, and Cemetery Authority) unless the employee serves solely as a Notary Public. (**08**) Any individual who is an Agent (active/inactive) serving in a fiduciary capacity under this CFPOA. (**09**) Upon the Principal's death, any individual or entity with a claim (the creditor) against the Principal's estate. (**10**) Any individual under eighteen (**18**) years or is incapacitated or incompetent. The Witnesses should be twenty-one (**21**) years of age or older.

Special Witness** If the Principal is a resident of a sanitarium, rest home, nursing home, boarding home, et cetera, it is highly beneficial that a patient advocate or ombudsman be one of the Witnesses while executing this CFPOA. **Legal Questions:** Consult the State laws or contact a licensed Attorney.

This page is intentionally left blank

This page is intentionally left blank

This page is intentionally left blank

CHAPTER 04

CHAPTER

04

Supporting Documents

CHAPTER 04

Overview

CHAPTER

04

Supporting Documents

Overview

The following documents are available if the Principal or Agent(s) needs them; these documents usually are optional. The design of these administrative support documents is to help fulfill the Power of Attorney (POA) goals and objectives.

For the Agent:

- **Acknowledgment of Appointment by Agent** **(01 Pages Total)**
  This document provides a record trail and transparency regarding who is the acting Agent; this document is optional (may be required) but highly recommended. This document is for administrative purposes.
- **Acknowledgment of Resignation by Agent** **(01 Pages Total)**
  This document provides a record trail and transparency regarding who is not the acting Agent; this document is optional (may be required) but highly recommended. This document is for administrative purposes.
- **Affidavit of Full Force and Effect** **(02 Pages Total)**
  This document provides a ready-made Affidavit if an interested third party needs further assurances that said POA is still valid and enforceable; this document is optional but highly recommended. This document is for administrative purposes.
- **Delegation of Agent's Powers** **(02 Pages Total)**
  This document provides a record trail and transparency regarding the delegation of power from one Agent to another Agent (Delegate); this document is optional (may be required) but highly recommended. This document is for administrative purposes.
- **Revocation of Delegate by Agent** **(01 Pages Total)**
  This document provides a ready-made Revocation of the Delegate if the Agent needs to revoke a Delegate; this document is optional but highly recommended. This document is for administrative purposes.
- **Co-Agent Power-Sharing Agreement** **(01 Pages Total)**
  This document provides a ready-made Agreement form for joint decisions issued by co-power sharing Agents; this document is optional but highly recommended. This document is for administrative purposes.

For the Principal:

- **Revocation in Whole** **(01 Pages Total)**
  This document provides a ready-made Revocation of the POA in whole if the Principal needs to revoke the POA; this document is optional but highly recommended. This document is for administrative purposes.
- **Revocation in Part(s)** **(01 Pages Total)**
  This document provides a ready-made Revocation of the POA in Part(s) if the Principal needs to delete a provision; this document is optional but highly recommended. This document is for administrative purposes.
- **Revocation of Agent** **(01 Pages Total)**
  This document provides a ready-made Revocation of the POA's Agent if the Principal needs to revoke an Agent; this document is optional but highly recommended. This document is for administrative purposes.
- **Revocation of Delegate by Principal** **(01 Pages Total)**
  This document provides a ready-made Revocation of the Delegate if the Principal needs to revoke a Delegate; this document is optional but highly recommended. This document is for administrative purposes.

CHAPTER

04

Supporting Documents

Overview

The following documents are available if the Protector or Delegate(s) needs them; these documents usually are optional. The design of these administrative support documents is to help fulfill the Power of Attorney (POA) goals and objectives.

For the Protector:

- **Acknowledgment of Appointment by Protector (01 Pages Total)**
  This document provides a record trail and transparency regarding who is the acting Protector; this document is optional (may be required) but highly recommended. This document is for administrative purposes.
- **Acknowledgment of Resignation by Protector (01 Pages Total)**
  This document provides a record trail and transparency regarding who is not the acting Protector; this document is optional (may be required) but highly recommended. This document is for administrative purposes.
- **Revocation of Agent by Protector (01 Pages Total)**
  This document provides a ready-made Revocation of the POA's Agent if the Protector needs to revoke an Agent; this document is optional but highly recommended. This document is for administrative purposes.
- **Revocation of Delegate by Protector (01 Pages Total)**
  This document provides a ready-made Revocation of the Delegate if the Protector needs to revoke a Delegate; this document is optional but highly recommended. This document is for administrative purposes.

For the Delegate:

- **Acknowledgment of Appointment by Delegate (01 Pages Total)**
  This document provides a record trail and transparency regarding who is the acting Delegate; this document is optional (may be required) but highly recommended. This document is for administrative purposes.
- **Acknowledgment of Resignation by Delegate (01 Pages Total)**
  This document provides a record trail and transparency regarding who is not the acting Delegate; this document is optional (may be required) but highly recommended. This document is for administrative purposes.

This page is intentionally left blank

Acknowledgment of Appointment by Agent

This page is intentionally blank so that reproduction (photocopy or print) of this page may occur by the Agent.

ACKNOWLEDGMENT OF APPOINTMENT BY AGENT

A: For purposes of brevity and consistency, the following abbreviation shall occur: ____________ shall be "**POA**," Attorney-In-Fact shall be "**Agent**," and Acknowledgment of Appointment by Agent shall be "**Appointment**."

B: The Principal requests that the acting Agent completes this Appointment; this Appointment is optional (may be required) but highly recommended.

C: The Agent has read carefully with fully understood all applicable/active provisions of this POA, especially **Acknowledgment by the Agent**.

D: By accepting or acting under this Appointment, the Agent assumes the fiduciary and other legal responsibilities of this role; with full knowledge of the responsibilities imposed on oneself and agrees to carry out the Principal's written instructions, terms, and wishes faithfully to the best of the Agent's ability.

E: The Agent agrees to keep all information (health, financial, relationship, or other personal matters) confidential and shall not disclose information to outsiders unless those individuals are relevant Third Parties that require said information to implement this POA.

TO: All persons, let it be known that the Agent,

Agent →			
	Full Legal Name:		**Signature:**
	Today's Date:		

In the presence of a Notary, the Agent has accepted the Appointment for the POA as an active Agent. The Agent understands the full import and meaning of this Appointment. The Agent affirms the following in the Notary's presence: (**01**) The Agent is at least eighteen (**18**) years or older. (**02**) The Agent is of sound and disposing mind (emotionally and mentally competent). (**03**) The Agent has the capacity with full memory or necessary mental faculties to understand and comprehend these actions. (**04**) The Agent willfully and voluntarily executes this Appointment. The Agent declares that this paragraph is true and correct under the Penalty of Perjury.

References to POA

The POA granting the Agent's authority, rights, and powers has the following date of execution:

Month of: ______ **Day of:** _______ **Year of:** ______ **← Date of execution of the POA**

A formal recording/filing (optional) of a true copy of the POA is with the following:

Public Records of:				
	Location's Name:		**Docket #**	
	Location's Address:		**Page #**	

UNDER THE LAWS OF ➔ STATE: ____________________, COUNTY: ______________

Before the Notary Public (the undersigned authority) comes forth, the Agent, with a sound/disposed mind, is eighteen (**18**) years or older. The Agent acknowledges having willfully and voluntarily dated and signed this Appointment (or ask/direct for such actions to occur) stated above in the Notary Public's presence. Furthermore, the Notary Public states that the Agent has provided a Government Issue identification card with a facial picture to prove identity. The Notary Public declares under the Penalty of Perjury that this paragraph is true and correct.

DIRECTION FOR NOTARY PUBLIC: The Notary Public shall verify the Agent's Identity with a Government Issue Picture I.D. The Notary Public must see the following: (**01**) True Original Copies of POA and (**02**) Agent Designation on the POA. If the Agent signs this Appointment but not in the presence of the Notary Public, then the Notary Public will not notarize or sign this Appointment.

Notary Public →				
	Full Legal Name:		**Signature & Seal :**	
	Location Name:			
	Address:		**Commission Number:**	
	Phone Number:			
	Today's Date:		**Commission Expires:**	

Acknowledgment of Resignation by Agent

This page is intentionally blank so that reproduction (photocopy or print) of this page may occur by the Agent.

ACKNOWLEDGMENT OF RESIGNATION BY AGENT

A: For purposes of brevity and consistency, the following abbreviation shall occur: ______________ shall be "**POA**," Attorney-In-Fact shall be "**Agent**," and Acknowledgment of Resignation by Agent shall be "**Resignation**."

B: The Principal requests that the acting Agent completes this Resignation; this Resignation is optional (may be required) but highly recommended.

C: The Agent agrees to keep all information (health, financial, relationship, or other personal matters) confidential and shall not disclose information to outsiders unless those individuals are relevant Third Parties that require said information to implement this POA.

TO: All persons, let it be known that the Agent,

Agent →			
	Full Legal Name:		Signature:
	Today's Date:		

The Agent understands the full import and meaning of this Resignation. The Agent affirms the following in the Notary's presence: (**01**) The Agent is at least eighteen (**18**) years or older. (**02**) The Agent is of sound and disposing mind (emotionally and mentally competent). (**03**) The Agent has the capacity with full memory or necessary mental faculties to understand and comprehend these actions. (**04**) The Agent willfully and voluntarily executes this Resignation. The Agent declares that this paragraph is true and correct under the Penalty of Perjury.

Agent's reason for Resignation

Directions: Please check "✓" the block and then initial the line "🖉" next to the selection below that best fits the Agent situation; select only (**01**) one option for each option is mutually exclusive to each other.

Check ↑	Initial ↑		Check ↑	Initial ↑		Check ↑	Initial ↑	
☐	______	**Resign**	☐	______	**Refuses**	☐	______	**Unable**

In the presence of a Notary, the Agent acknowledges their resignation status (stated above) as to their inability to act for the Principal; thus, the Agent relinquishes their role and all rights thereof as the Agent in reference to the POA (stated below). The Agent declares that this paragraph is true and correct under the Penalty of Perjury.

References to POA

The POA from which the Agent is resigning has the following date of execution:

Month of: ______ **Day of:** ______ **Year of:** ______ ← **Date of execution of the POA**

A formal recording/filing (optional) of a true copy of the POA is with the following:

Public Records of:				
	Location's Name:		Docket #	
	Location's Address:		Page #	

UNDER THE LAWS OF ➔ STATE: ____________________, COUNTY: ____________________

Before the Notary Public (the undersigned authority) comes forth, the Agent, with a sound/disposed mind, is eighteen (**18**) years or older. The Agent acknowledges having willfully and voluntarily dated and signed this Resignation (or ask/direct for such actions to occur) stated above in the Notary Public's presence. Furthermore, the Notary Public states that the Agent has provided a Government Issue identification card with a facial picture to prove identity. The Notary Public declares under the Penalty of Perjury that this paragraph is true and correct.

DIRECTION FOR NOTARY PUBLIC: The Notary Public shall verify the Agent's Identity with a Government Issue Picture I.D. If the Agent signs this Resignation but not in the presence of the Notary Public, then the Notary Public will not notarize or sign this Resignation.

Notary Public →				
	Full Legal Name:		Signature & Seal :	
	Location Name:			
	Address:			
	Phone Number:		Commission Number:	
	Today's Date:		Commission Expires:	

Affidavit of Full Force and Effect

This page is intentionally blank so that reproduction (photocopy or print) of this page may occur by the Agent.

AFFIDAVIT OF FULL FORCE AND EFFECT

For purposes of brevity and consistency, the following abbreviation shall occur: ______________________ shall be "**POA**," Attorney-In-Fact shall be "**Agent**," Company, Organization, or Individual(s) shall be "**Third Party**," and Affidavit of Full Force and Effect shall be "**Affidavit**."

TO: All persons, let it be known that the Agent,

Agent →				
Full Legal Name:				
Current Address:				
Phone Number:		**Email:**		
Residence:	**County:**		**State :**	

Having now duly sworn, deposes, and says that the:

Principal →				
Full Legal Name:				
Current Address:				
Phone Number:		**Email:**		
Residence:	**County:**		**State :**	

The Principal, in writing, appointed the above individual as the Principal true and lawful Agent; attached is a true copy of the POA. In the presence of a Notary, the Agent has executed this Affidavit. The Agent understands the full import and meaning of this Affidavit. The Agent affirms the following in the Notary's presence: (**01**) The Agent is at least eighteen (**18**) years or older. (**02**) The Agent is of sound and disposing mind (emotionally and mentally competent) to make or request this Affidavit. (**03**) The Agent has the capacity with full memory or necessary mental faculties to understand and comprehend these actions. (**04**) The Agent willfully and voluntarily executes this Affidavit for inducing the Third Party as stated below.

References to POA

The POA granting the Agent's authority, rights, and powers has the following date of execution:

Month of: ______ **Day of:** _______ **Year of:** ______ **← Date of execution of the POA**

A formal recording/filing (optional) of a true copy of the POA is with the following:

Public Records of:			
Location's Name:		**Docket #**	
Location's Address:		**Page #**	

Name of Third Party

____

Name of Third Party here ↑

- The Agent agrees to notify the above-stated Third Party in writing immediately if this POA has been revoked or otherwise terminated by the following: (**01**) Revocation by the Principal. (**02**) The Principal is dead. (**03**) A court has issued a court order to terminate the Principal's POA. If Durable Provision(s) are not active or applicable, the following: (**04**) The Principal is functioning non-socially. (**05**) The Principal is incapacitated. (**06**) The Principal is incompetent.
- The Third Party agrees to exchange consideration based on the attached POA. The Agent indemnifies and holds harmless the Third Party, its parent company, subsidiaries, affiliates, and their predecessors, successors, and employees for any loss, damage, or expense it may sustain due to the failure by the Agent to notify the Third Party as described in the paragraph above.
- In the Agent's capacity, for the acceptance of delivery of the POA, as executed by the Principal. The Agent intends to execute this Affidavit with full knowledge that it will be utilized and relied upon to accept the delivery of instrument(s) and pay good and valuable consideration.

Initial of Notary Public: ____________ **Initial of Agent:** ____________

Acknowledgment and Attestation

TO: All persons, let it be known that the Agent,

Agent →		
Full Legal Name:		**Signature:**
Today's Date:		

The Agent states, to the best of their knowledge, the following: (**01**) Receive no notice of revocation of POA. (**02**) The Principal is currently alive, not dead. (**03**) Absent an active Durable Provisions, the Principal is not functioning non-socially, incapacitated, or incompetent. (**04**) The Principal has not revoked, terminated, suspended, or repudiated the POA. (**05**) The POA is currently in full force and effect, executed when the Principal was in a Healthy State. Having read the statements above, the Agent swears, affirms, and declares under the Penalties of Perjury that the content of this Affidavit is true and correct.

UNDER THE LAWS OF → STATE:____________________, COUNTY:____________________

Before the Notary Public (the undersigned authority) comes forth, the Agent, with a sound/disposed mind, is eighteen (**18**) years or older. The Agent acknowledges having willfully and voluntarily dated and signed this Affidavit (or ask/direct for such actions to occur) stated above in the Notary Public's presence. Furthermore, the Notary Public states that the Agent has provided a Government Issue identification card with a facial picture to prove identity. The Notary Public declares under the Penalty of Perjury that this paragraph is true and correct.

DIRECTION FOR NOTARY PUBLIC: The Notary Public shall verify Agent's Identity with a Government Issue Picture I.D. If the Agent signs this Affidavit but not in the presence of the Notary Public, then the Notary Public will not notarize or sign this Affidavit.

Notary Public →			
Full Legal Name:		**Signature & Seal :**	
Location Name:			
Address:			
		Commission Number:	
Phone Number:			
Today's Date:		**Commission Expires:**	

This page is intentionally left blank

Delegation of Agent's Powers

This page is intentionally blank so that reproduction (photocopy or print) of this page may occur by the Agent.

DELEGATION OF AGENT'S POWERS

A: For purposes of brevity and consistency, the following abbreviation shall occur: ____________ shall be "**POA**," Subservient Agent shall be "**Delegate**," and Delegation of Agent's Powers shall be "**DOAP**."

B: The Agent has read carefully with fully understood all applicable/active provisions of this POA, especially **Acknowledgment by the Agent,** and has imparted this understanding to the Delegate.

C: By accepting or acting under this DOAP, the Agent and Delegate assumes the fiduciary and other legal responsibilities of this role, with full knowledge of the responsibilities imposed on oneself and agree to carry out the Principal's written instructions, terms, and wishes faithfully to the best of the Agent's and Delegate's ability.

D: The Agent and Delegate agree to keep all information (health, financial, relationship, or other personal matters) confidential and shall not disclose information to outsiders unless those individuals are relevant Third Parties that require said information to implement this POA.

TO: All persons, let it be known that the Agent,

Agent →			
	Full Legal Name:		Signature:
	Today's Date:		

In the presence of a Notary, the Agent has executed this DOAP. The Agent understands the full import and meaning of this DOAP. The Agent affirms the following in the Notary's presence: (**01**) The Agent is at least eighteen (**18**) years or older. (**02**) The Agent is of sound and disposing mind (emotionally and mentally competent). (**03**) The Agent has the capacity with full memory or necessary mental faculties to understand and comprehend these actions. (**04**) The Agent willfully and voluntarily executes this DOAP. The Agent declares that this paragraph is true and correct under the Penalty of Perjury.

The Agent Authorization for a Delegate to act on their behalf

The Agent has bestowed or referred some of their power /responsibility to the following Delegate as named below:

____

Name of Delegate here ↑ (Must be an Approved Agent who appears within the POA).

References to POA

The POA that the Agent is referring to has the following date of execution:

Month of: _______ **Day of:** _______ **Year of:** _____ ← **Date of execution of the POA**

A formal recording/filing (optional) of a true copy of the POA is with the following:

Public Records of:				
	Location's Name:		Docket #	
	Location's Address:		Page #	

Required: The Agent is delegating the following powers to the Delegate to perform and act in the Agent's name, place, and stead for the Principal's benefit.

Specify in Detail		Must be Type

Initial of Notary Public: __________ **Initial of Agent:** __________

UNDER THE LAWS OF ➔ STATE: ____________________, COUNTY: ____________________

Before the Notary Public (the undersigned authority) comes forth, the Agent, with a sound/disposed mind, is eighteen (**18**) years or older. The Agent acknowledges having willfully and voluntarily dated and signed this DOAP (or ask/direct for such actions to occur) stated above in the Notary Public's presence. Furthermore, the Notary Public states that the Agent has provided a Government Issue identification card with a facial picture to prove identity. The Notary Public declares under the Penalty of Perjury that this paragraph is true and correct.

DIRECTION FOR NOTARY PUBLIC: The Notary Public shall verify the Agent's Identity with a Government Issue Picture I.D. The Notary Public must see the following: (**01**) True Original Copies of POA and (**02**) Agent and Delegate designation on the POA. If the Agent signs this DOAP but not in the presence of the Notary Public, then the Notary Public will not notarize or sign this DOAP.

Notary Public →				
	Full Legal Name:		**Signature & Seal :**	
	Location Name:			
	Address:		**Commission Number:**	
	Phone Number:			
	Today's Date:		**Commission Expires:**	

Initial of Notary Public: ____________ **Initial of Agent:** ____________

This page is intentionally left blank

Revocation of Delegate by Agent

This page is intentionally blank so that reproduction (photocopy or print) of this page may occur by the Agent.

REVOCATION OF DELEGATE BY AGENT

For purposes of brevity and consistency, the following abbreviation shall occur: ______________________ shall be "**POA**," Delegation of Agent's Power shall be "**DOAP**," Attorney-In-Fact shall be "**Agent**," subservient Agent shall be "**Delegate**," and Revocation of Delegate by Agent shall be "**Revocation**."

TO: All persons, let it be known that the Agent,

Agent →			
Full Legal Name:		Signature:	
Today's Date:			

In the presence of a Notary, the Agent has executed this Revocation. The Agent understands the full import and meaning of this Revocation. The Agent affirms the following in the Notary's presence: (**01**) The Agent is at least eighteen (**18**) years or older. (**02**) The Agent is of sound and disposing mind (emotionally and mentally competent). (**03**) The Agent has the capacity with full memory or necessary mental faculties to understand and comprehend these actions. (**04**) The Agent willfully and voluntarily executes this Revocation. The Agent declares that this paragraph is true and correct under the Penalty of Perjury.

References to DOAP

The DOAP that the Agent is referring to has the following date of execution:

Month of: ________ **Day of:** ________ **Year of:** ________ ← **Date of execution of the DOAP**

A formal recording/filing (optional) of a true copy of the DOAP is with the following:

Public Records of:				
Location's Name:		Docket #	
Location's Address:		Page #	

The Agent immediately revokes the Delegate's rights, power, and authority (as mentioned below).

Delegate →				
Full Legal Name:				
Current Address:				
Phone Number:		Email:		
Residence:	County:		State :	

Optional: The reason for this Revocation of Delegate is as follows:

Specify in Detail	

UNDER THE LAWS OF → STATE: ______________________, COUNTY: ______________________

Before the Notary Public (the undersigned authority) comes forth, the Agent, with a sound/disposed mind, is eighteen (**18**) years or older. The Agent acknowledges having willfully and voluntarily dated and signed this Revocation (or ask/direct for such actions to occur) stated above in the Notary Public's presence. Furthermore, the Notary Public states that the Agent has provided a Government Issue identification card with a facial picture to prove identity. The Notary Public declares under the Penalty of Perjury that this paragraph is true and correct.

DIRECTION FOR NOTARY PUBLIC: The Notary Public shall verify the Agent's Identity with a Government Issue Picture I.D. The Notary Public must see the following: (**01**) True Original Copies of DOAP and (**02**) Agent and Delegate designation on the DOAP. If the Agent signs this Revocation but not in the presence of the Notary Public, then the Notary Public will not notarize or sign this Revocation.

Notary Public →			
Full Legal Name:		Signature & Seal :	
Location Name:			
Address:			
Phone Number:		Commission Number:	
Today's Date:		Commission Expires:	

Co-Agent Power-Sharing Agreement

This page is intentionally blank so that reproduction (photocopy or print) of this page may occur by the Agent(s).

CO-AGENT POWER-SHARING AGREEMENT

For purposes of brevity and consistency, the following abbreviation shall occur: ______________ shall be "**POA**," Attorney-In-Fact shall be "**Agent**," and Co-Agent Power Sharing Agreement shall be "**Agreement**."

TO: All persons, let it be known that the Agent(s) as stated below are Co-Agent:

Agent →

Full Legal Name:			
Current Address:			
Phone Number:		**Email:**	
Residence:	**County:**		**State :**

&

Agent →

Full Legal Name:			
Current Address:			
Phone Number:		**Email:**	
Residence:	**County:**		**State :**

The Agent(s) shall have the authority and power to make joint decisions on the Principal behalf in a co-power sharing arrangement. Co-power sharing involves the Agent(s) making and implementing decisions together. Every joint decision must be in writing with both Agent(s) having signed off as approving such decisions.

References to POA

The POA granting the Agent(s) authority, rights, and powers has the following date of execution:

Month of: _______ **Day of:** ________ **Year of:** ______ ← **Date of execution of the POA**

A formal recording/filing (optional) of a true copy of the POA is with the following:

Public Records of:

Location's Name:		**Docket #**	
Location's Address:		**Page #**	

Agreement: The Agent(s) agrees to the following course of action concerning the Principal's Property or Affairs:

Specify in Detail		Must be Type

Acknowledgment and Attestation

UNDER THE LAWS OF ➔ STATE: ____________________, COUNTY: ____________________

The Agent(s) understand the full import and meaning of this Agreement. The Agent(s) affirms the following in their joint presence: (**01**) The Agent(s) is at least eighteen (**18**) years or older. (**02**) The Agent(s) is of sound and disposing mind (emotionally and mentally competent) to make or request this Agreement. (**03**) The Agent(s) has the capacity with full memory or necessary mental faculties to understand and comprehend these actions. (**04**) The Agent(s) willfully and voluntarily executes this Agreement. The Agent(s) declares under the Penalty of Perjury that this paragraph is true and correct.

Agent →

Full Legal Name:		**Signature:**
Today's Date:		

&

Agent →

Full Legal Name:		**Signature:**
Today's Date:		

Revocation in Whole

This page is intentionally blank so that reproduction (photocopy or print) of this page may occur by the Principal.

REVOCATION IN WHOLE

For purposes of brevity and consistency, the following abbreviation shall occur: ____________________
shall be "**POA**," Attorney-In-Fact shall be "**Agent**," and Revocation in Whole shall be "**Revocation**."

TO: All persons, let it be known that the Principal,

Principal →	Full Legal Name:		Signature:
	Today's Date:		

In the presence of a Notary, the Principal has executed this Revocation. The Principal understands the full import and meaning of this Revocation. The Principal affirms the following in the Notary's presence: (**01**) The Principal is at least eighteen (**18**) years or older. (**02**) The Principal is of sound and disposing mind (emotionally and mentally competent). (**03**) The Principal has the capacity with full memory or necessary mental faculties to understand and comprehend these actions. (**04**) The Principal willfully and voluntarily executes this Revocation. The Principal declares that this paragraph is true and correct under the Penalty of Perjury.

References to POA

The POA that the Principal is referring to has the following date of execution:

Month of: ______ **Day of:** ______ **Year of:** ______ **← Date of execution of the POA**

A formal recording/filing (optional) of a true copy of the POA is with the following:

Public Records of:	Location's Name:		Docket #	
	Location's Address:		Page #	

The Principal is revoking the POA (in whole) as referenced above, effective immediately.

Specify in Detail	**Optional:** The reason for this Revocation is as follows:

UNDER THE LAWS OF → STATE: ____________________, COUNTY: ____________________

Before the Notary Public (the undersigned authority) comes forth, the Principal, with a sound/disposed mind, is eighteen (**18**) years or older. The Principal acknowledges having willfully and voluntarily dated and signed this Revocation (or ask/direct for such actions to occur) stated above in the Notary Public's presence. Furthermore, the Notary Public states that the Principal has provided a Government Issue identification card with a facial picture to prove identity. The Notary Public declares under the Penalty of Perjury that this paragraph is true and correct.

DIRECTION FOR NOTARY PUBLIC: The Notary Public shall verify the Principal's Identity with a Government Issue Picture I.D. If the Principal signs this Revocation but not in the presence of the Notary Public, then the Notary Public will not notarize or sign this Revocation.

Notary Public →	Full Legal Name:		Signature & Seal :	
	Location Name:			
	Address:			
	Phone Number:		Commission Number:	
	Today's Date:		Commission Expires:	

Revocation in Part(s)

This page is intentionally blank so that reproduction (photocopy or print) of this page may occur by the Principal.

REVOCATION IN PART(S)

For purposes of brevity and consistency, the following abbreviation shall occur: ____________________ shall be "**POA**," Attorney-In-Fact shall be "**Agent**," and Revocation in Part(s) shall be "**Revocation**."

TO: All persons, let it be known that the Principal,

Principal →		
Full Legal Name:		**Signature:**
Today's Date:		

In the presence of a Notary, the Principal has executed this Revocation. The Principal understands the full import and meaning of this Revocation. The Principal affirms the following in the Notary's presence: (**01**) The Principal is at least eighteen (**18**) years or older. (**02**) The Principal is of sound and disposing mind (emotionally and mentally competent). (**03**) The Principal has the capacity with full memory or necessary mental faculties to understand and comprehend these actions. (**04**) The Principal willfully and voluntarily executes this Revocation. The Principal declares that this paragraph is true and correct under the Penalty of Perjury.

References to POA

The POA that the Principal is referring to has the following date of execution:

Month of: ______ **Day of:** ______ **Year of:** ______ ← **Date of execution of the POA**

A formal recording/filing (optional) of a true copy of the POA is with the following:

Public Records of:			
Location's Name:		**Docket #**	
Location's Address:		**Page #**	

Required: The Principal revokes this POA in Part(s) as referenced above, effective immediately.

Specify in Detail		**Preferably Type**

UNDER THE LAWS OF → STATE: ____________________, COUNTY: ____________________

Before the Notary Public (the undersigned authority) comes forth, the Principal, with a sound/disposed mind, is eighteen (**18**) years or older. The Principal acknowledges having willfully and voluntarily dated and signed this Revocation (or ask/direct for such actions to occur) stated above in the Notary Public's presence. Furthermore, the Notary Public states that the Principal has provided a Government Issue identification card with a facial picture to prove identity. The Notary Public declares under the Penalty of Perjury that this paragraph is true and correct.

DIRECTION FOR NOTARY PUBLIC: The Notary Public shall verify the Principal's Identity with a Government Issue Picture I.D. If the Principal signs this Revocation but not in the presence of the Notary Public, then the Notary Public will not notarize or sign this Revocation.

Notary Public →		
Full Legal Name:		**Signature & Seal :**
Location Name:		
Address:		
Phone Number:		**Commission Number:**
Today's Date:		**Commission Expires:**

Revocation of Agent

This page is intentionally blank so that reproduction (photocopy or print) of this page may occur by the Principal.

REVOCATION OF AGENT

For purposes of brevity and consistency, the following abbreviation shall occur: ______________________ shall be "**POA**," Attorney-In-Fact shall be "**Agent**," and Revocation of Agent shall be "**Revocation**."

TO: All persons, let it be known that the Principal,

Principal →

Full Legal Name:		**Signature:**
Today's Date:		

In the presence of a Notary, the Principal has executed this Revocation. The Principal understands the full import and meaning of this Revocation. The Principal affirms the following in the Notary's presence: (**01**) The Principal is at least eighteen (**18**) years or older. (**02**) The Principal is of sound and disposing mind (emotionally and mentally competent). (**03**) The Principal has the capacity with full memory or necessary mental faculties to understand and comprehend these actions. (**04**) The Principal willfully and voluntarily executes this Revocation. The Principal declares that this paragraph is true and correct under the Penalty of Perjury.

References to POA

The POA that the Principal is referring to has the following date of execution:

Month of: ______ **Day of:** _______ **Year of:** ______ **← Date of execution of the POA**

A formal recording/filing (optional) of a true copy of the POA is with the following:

Public Records of:

Location's Name:		**Docket #**	
Location's Address:		**Page #**	

The Principal immediately revokes the Agent's rights, power, and authority (as mentioned below).

Agent →

Full Legal Name:			
Current Address:			
Phone Number:		**Email:**	
Residence:	**County:**		**State :**

Optional: The reason for this Revocation of Agent is as follows:

Specify in Detail

UNDER THE LAWS OF → STATE: ____________________, COUNTY: ____________________

Before the Notary Public (the undersigned authority) comes forth, the Principal, with a sound/disposed mind, is eighteen (**18**) years or older. The Principal acknowledges having willfully and voluntarily dated and signed this Revocation (or ask/direct for such actions to occur) stated above in the Notary Public's presence. Furthermore, the Notary Public states that the Principal has provided a Government Issue identification card with a facial picture to prove identity. The Notary Public declares under the Penalty of Perjury that this paragraph is true and correct.

DIRECTION FOR NOTARY PUBLIC: The Notary Public shall verify the Principal's Identity with a Government Issue Picture I.D. If the Principal signs this Revocation but not in the presence of the Notary Public, then the Notary Public will not notarize or sign this Revocation.

Notary Public →

Full Legal Name:		**Signature & Seal :**	
Location Name:			
Address:		**Commission Number:**	
Phone Number:			
Today's Date:		**Commission Expires:**	

Revocation of Delegate by Principal

This page is intentionally blank so that reproduction (photocopy or print) of this page may occur by the Principal.

REVOCATION OF DELEGATE BY PRINCIPAL

For purposes of brevity and consistency, the following abbreviation shall occur: ______ shall be "**POA**," Delegation of Agent's Power shall be "**DOAP**," Attorney-In-Fact shall be "**Agent**," subservient Agent shall be "**Delegate**," and Revocation of Delegate by Principal shall be "**Revocation**."

TO: All persons, let it be known that the Principal,

Principal →		
Full Legal Name:		Signature:
Today's Date:		

In the presence of a Notary, the Principal has executed this Revocation. The Principal understands the full import and meaning of this Revocation. The Principal affirms the following in the Notary's presence: (**01**) The Principal is at least eighteen (**18**) years or older. (**02**) The Principal is of sound and disposing mind (emotionally and mentally competent). (**03**) The Principal has the capacity with full memory or necessary mental faculties to understand and comprehend these actions. (**04**) The Principal willfully and voluntarily executes this Revocation. The Principal declares that this paragraph is true and correct under the Penalty of Perjury.

References to DOAP

The DOAP that the Principal is referring to has the following date of execution:

Month of: ______ **Day of:** ______ **Year of:** ______ ← **Date of execution of the DOAP**

A formal recording/filing (optional) of a true copy of the DOAP is with the following:

Public Records of:				
	Location's Name:		Docket #	
	Location's Address:		Page #	

The Principal immediately revokes the Delegate's rights, power, and authority (as mentioned below).

Delegate →				
Full Legal Name:				
Current Address:				
Phone Number:		Email:		
Residence:	County:		State :	

Optional: The reason for this Revocation of Delegate is as follows:

Specify in Detail	

UNDER THE LAWS OF → STATE: ______________, COUNTY: ______________

Before the Notary Public (the undersigned authority) comes forth, the Principal, with a sound/disposed mind, is eighteen (**18**) years or older. The Principal acknowledges having willfully and voluntarily dated and signed this Revocation (or ask/direct for such actions to occur) stated above in the Notary Public's presence. Furthermore, the Notary Public states that the Principal has provided a Government Issue identification card with a facial picture to prove identity. The Notary Public declares under the Penalty of Perjury that this paragraph is true and correct.

DIRECTION FOR NOTARY PUBLIC: The Notary Public shall verify the Principal's Identity with a Government Issue Picture I.D. The Notary Public must see the following: (**01**) True Original Copies of DOAP and (**02**) Principal designation on the POA mentioned in the DOAP. If the Principal signs this Revocation but not in the presence of the Notary Public, then the Notary Public will not notarize or sign this Revocation.

Notary Public →			
Full Legal Name:		Signature & Seal :	
Location Name:			
Address:			
Phone Number:		Commission Number:	
Today's Date:		Commission Expires:	

Acknowledgment of Appointment by Protector

This page is intentionally blank so that reproduction (photocopy or print) of this page may occur by the Protector.

ACKNOWLEDGMENT OF APPOINTMENT BY PROTECTOR

A: For purposes of brevity and consistency, the following abbreviation shall occur: Durable Protecting Power of Attorney shall be "**POA**," and Acknowledgment of Appointment shall be "**Appointment**."

B: The Principal requests that the acting Protector completes this Appointment; this Appointment is optional (may be required) but highly recommended.

C: The Protector has read carefully with fully understood all applicable/active provisions of this POA, especially **Acknowledgment by the Agent**.

D: By accepting or acting under this Appointment, the Protector assumes the fiduciary and other legal responsibilities of this role; with full knowledge of the responsibilities imposed on oneself and agrees to carry out the Principal duties faithfully to the best of the Protector's ability.

E: The Protector agrees to keep all information (health, financial, relationship, or other personal matters) confidential and shall not disclose information to outsiders unless those individuals are relevant Third Parties that require said information to implement this POA.

TO: All persons, let it be known that the Protector,

Protector →			
	Full Legal Name:		Signature:
	Today's Date:		

In the presence of a Notary, the Protector has accepted the Appointment for the POA as an active Protector. The Protector understands the full import and meaning of this Appointment. The Protector affirms the following in the Notary's presence: (**01**) The Protector is at least eighteen (**18**) years or older. (**02**) The Protector is of sound and disposing mind (emotionally and mentally competent). (**03**) The Protector has the capacity with full memory or necessary mental faculties to understand and comprehend these actions. (**04**) The Protector willfully and voluntarily executes this Appointment. The Protector declares that this paragraph is true and correct under the Penalty of Perjury.

References to POA

The POA granting the Protector's authority, rights, and powers has the following date of execution:

Month of: ______ **Day of:** _______ **Year of:** _____ ← **Date of execution of the POA**

A formal recording/filing (optional) of a true copy of the POA is with the following:

Public Records of:				
	Location's Name:		Docket #	
	Location's Address:		Page #	

UNDER THE LAWS OF → STATE: ____________________, COUNTY: ________________

Before the Notary Public (the undersigned authority) comes forth, the Protector, with a sound/disposed mind, is eighteen (**18**) years or older. The Protector acknowledges having willfully and voluntarily dated and signed this Appointment (or ask/direct for such actions to occur) stated above in the Notary Public's presence. Furthermore, the Notary Public states that the Protector has provided a Government Issue identification card with a facial picture to prove identity. The Notary Public declares under the Penalty of Perjury that this paragraph is true and correct.

DIRECTION FOR NOTARY PUBLIC: The Notary Public shall verify the Protector's Identity with a Government Issue Picture I.D. The Notary Public must see the following: (**01**) True Original Copies of POA and (**02**) Protector Designation on the POA. If the Protector signs this Appointment but not in the presence of the Notary Public, then the Notary Public will not notarize or sign this Appointment.

Notary Public →				
	Full Legal Name:		Signature & Seal :	
	Location Name:			
	Address:			
	Phone Number:		Commission Number:	
	Today's Date:		Commission Expires:	

Acknowledgment of Resignation by Protector

This page is intentionally blank so that reproduction (photocopy or print) of this page may occur by the Protector.

ACKNOWLEDGMENT OF RESIGNATION BY PROTECTOR

A: For purposes of brevity and consistency, the following abbreviation shall occur: Durable Protecting Power of Attorney shall be "**POA**," and Acknowledgment of Resignation by Protector shall be "**Resignation**."

B: The Principal requests that the acting Protector completes this Resignation; this Resignation is optional (may be required) but highly recommended.

C: The Protector agrees to keep all information (health, financial, relationship, or other personal matters) confidential and shall not disclose information to outsiders unless those individuals are relevant Third Parties that require said information to implement this POA.

TO: All persons, let it be known that the Protector,

Protector →		
Full Legal Name:		**Signature:**
Today's Date:		

The Protector understands the full import and meaning of this Resignation. The Protector affirms the following in the Notary's presence: (**01**) The Protector is at least eighteen (**18**) years or older. (**02**) The Protector is of sound and disposing mind (emotionally and mentally competent). (**03**) The Protector has the capacity with full memory or necessary mental faculties to understand and comprehend these actions. (**04**) The Protector willfully and voluntarily executes this Resignation. The Protector declares that this paragraph is true and correct under the Penalty of Perjury.

Protector's reason for Resignation

Directions: Please check "✓" the block and then initial the line "✎" next to the selection below that best fits the Protector situation; select only (**01**) one option for each option is mutually exclusive to each other.

☐	____	**Resign**	☐	____	**Refuses**	☐	____	**Unable**
Check ↑	Initial ↑		Check ↑	Initial ↑		Check ↑	Initial ↑	

In the presence of a Notary, the Protector acknowledges their resignation status (stated above) as to their inability to act for the Principal; thus, the Protector relinquishes their role and all rights thereof as the Protector in reference to the POA (stated below). The Protector declares that this paragraph is true and correct under the Penalty of Perjury.

References to POA

The POA from which the Protector is resigning has the following date of execution:

Month of: ______ **Day of:** ______ **Year of:** ______ **← Date of execution of the POA**

A formal recording/filing (optional) of a true copy of the POA is with the following:

Public Records of:			
Location's Name:		**Docket #**	
Location's Address:		**Page #**	

UNDER THE LAWS OF ➔ STATE: ____________________, COUNTY: ____________________

Before the Notary Public (the undersigned authority) comes forth, the Protector, with a sound/disposed mind, is eighteen (**18**) years or older. The Protector acknowledges having willfully and voluntarily dated and signed this Resignation (or ask/direct for such actions to occur) stated above in the Notary Public's presence. Furthermore, the Notary Public states that the Protector has provided a Government Issue identification card with a facial picture to prove identity. The Notary Public declares under the Penalty of Perjury that this paragraph is true and correct.

DIRECTION FOR NOTARY PUBLIC: The Notary Public shall verify the Protector's Identity with a Government Issue Picture I.D. If the Protector signs this Resignation but not in the presence of the Notary Public, then the Notary Public will not notarize or sign this Resignation.

Notary Public →			
Full Legal Name:		**Signature & Seal :**	
Location Name:			
Address:			
Phone Number:		**Commission Number:**	
Today's Date:		**Commission Expires:**	

Revocation of Agent by Protector

This page is intentionally blank so that reproduction (photocopy or print) of this page may occur by the Protector.

REVOCATION OF AGENT BY PROTECTOR

For purposes of brevity and consistency, the following abbreviation shall occur: ____________________ shall be "**POA**," Attorney-In-Fact shall be "**Agent**," and Revocation of Agent by Protector shall be "**Revocation**."

TO: All persons, let it be known that the Protector,

Protector →

Full Legal Name:		Signature:
Today's Date:		

In the presence of a Notary, the Protector has executed this Revocation. The Protector understands the full import and meaning of this Revocation. The Protector affirms the following in the Notary's presence: (**01**) The Protector is at least eighteen (**18**) years or older. (**02**) The Protector is of sound and disposing mind (emotionally and mentally competent). (**03**) The Protector has the capacity with full memory or necessary mental faculties to understand and comprehend these actions. (**04**) The Protector willfully and voluntarily executes this Revocation. The Protector declares that this paragraph is true and correct under the Penalty of Perjury.

References to POA

The POA that the Protector is referring to has the following date of execution:

Month of: ______ **Day of:** ______ **Year of:** ______ **← Date of execution of the POA**

A formal recording/filing (optional) of a true copy of the POA is with the following:

Public Records of:

Location's Name:		Docket #	
Location's Address:		Page #	

The Protector immediately revokes the Agent's rights, power, and authority (as mentioned below).

Agent →

Full Legal Name:			
Current Address:			
Phone Number:		Email:	
Residence:	County:	State :	

Required: The Protector states that the above name Agent violates their fiduciary duties due to the following:

Specify in Detail		Must be Type

UNDER THE LAWS OF → STATE: ____________________, COUNTY: ____________________

Before the Notary Public (the undersigned authority) comes forth, the Protector, with a sound/disposed mind, is eighteen (**18**) years or older. The Protector acknowledges having willfully and voluntarily dated and signed this Revocation (or ask/direct for such actions to occur) stated above in the Notary Public's presence. Furthermore, the Notary Public states that the Protector has provided a Government Issue identification card with a facial picture to prove identity. The Notary Public declares under the Penalty of Perjury that this paragraph is true and correct.

DIRECTION FOR NOTARY PUBLIC: The Notary Public shall verify the Protector's Identity with a Government Issue Picture I.D. The Notary Public must see the following: (**01**) True Original Copies of POA and (**02**) Protector and Agent designation on the POA. If the Protector signs this Revocation but not in the presence of the Notary Public, then the Notary Public will not notarize or sign this Revocation.

Notary Public →

Full Legal Name:		Signature & Seal :	
Location Name:			
Address:		Commission Number:	
Phone Number:			
Today's Date:		Commission Expires:	

Revocation of Delegate by Protector

This page is intentionally blank so that reproduction (photocopy or print) of this page may occur by the Protector.

REVOCATION OF DELEGATE BY PROTECTOR

For purposes of brevity and consistency, the following abbreviation shall occur: ____________ shall be "**POA**," Delegation of Agent's Power shall be "**DOAP**," Attorney-In-Fact shall be "**Agent**," subservient Agent shall be "**Delegate**," and Revocation of Delegate by Protector shall be "**Revocation**."

TO: All persons, let it be known that the Protector,

Protector →			
	Full Legal Name:		**Signature:**
	Today's Date:		

In the presence of a Notary, the Protector has executed this Revocation. The Protector understands the full import and meaning of this Revocation. The Protector affirms the following in the Notary's presence: (**01**) The Protector is at least eighteen (**18**) years or older. (**02**) The Protector is of sound and disposing mind (emotionally and mentally competent). (**03**) The Protector has the capacity with full memory or necessary mental faculties to understand and comprehend these actions. (**04**) The Protector willfully and voluntarily executes this Revocation. The Protector declares that this paragraph is true and correct under the Penalty of Perjury.

References to DOAP

The DOAP that the Protector is referring to has the following date of execution:

Month of: ______ **Day of:** _______ **Year of:** ______ **← Date of execution of the DOAP**

A formal recording/filing (optional) of a true copy of the DOAP is with the following:

Public Records of:				
	Location's Name:		**Docket #**	
	Location's Address:		**Page #**	

The Protector immediately revokes the Delegate's rights, power, and authority (as mentioned below).

Delegate →				
	Full Legal Name:			
	Current Address:			
	Phone Number:		**Email:**	
	Residence:	**County:**		**State :**

Required: The Protector states that the above name Delegate violates their fiduciary duties due to the following:

Specify in Detail		**Must be Type**

UNDER THE LAWS OF → STATE: ________________, COUNTY: ________________

Before the Notary Public (the undersigned authority) comes forth, the Protector, with a sound/disposed mind, is eighteen (**18**) years or older. The Protector acknowledges having willfully and voluntarily dated and signed this Revocation (or ask/direct for such actions to occur) stated above in the Notary Public's presence. Furthermore, the Notary Public states that the Protector has provided a Government Issue identification card with a facial picture to prove identity. The Notary Public declares under the Penalty of Perjury that this paragraph is true and correct.

DIRECTION FOR NOTARY PUBLIC: The Notary Public shall verify the Protector's Identity with a Government Issue Picture I.D. The Notary Public must see the following: (**01**) True Original Copies of DOAP and (**02**) Protector designation on the POA mentioned in the DOAP. If the Protector signs this Revocation but not in the presence of the Notary Public, then the Notary Public will not notarize or sign this Revocation.

Notary Public →				
	Full Legal Name:		**Signature & Seal :**	
	Location Name:			
	Address:			
	Phone Number:		**Commission Number:**	
	Today's Date:		**Commission Expires:**	

Acknowledgment of Appointment by Delegate

This page is intentionally blank so that reproduction (photocopy or print) of this page may occur by the Delegate.

ACKNOWLEDGMENT OF APPOINTMENT BY DELEGATE

A: For purposes of brevity and consistency, the following abbreviation shall occur: ____________ shall be "**POA**," Delegation of Agent's Power shall be "**DOAP**," Subservient Agent shall be "**Delegate**," and Acknowledgment of Appointment by Delegate shall be "**Appointment**."

B: The Principal requests that the acting Delegate completes this Appointment; this Appointment is optional (may be required) but highly recommended.

C: The Delegate has read carefully with fully understood all applicable/active provisions of this POA, especially **Acknowledgment by the Agent**.

D: By accepting or acting under this Appointment, the Delegate assumes the fiduciary and other legal responsibilities of this role; with full knowledge of the responsibilities imposed on oneself and agrees to carry out the **Principal**'s written instructions, terms, and wishes faithfully to the best of the Delegate's ability.

E: The Delegate agrees to keep all information (health, financial, relationship, or other personal matters) confidential and shall not disclose information to outsiders unless those individuals are relevant Third Parties that require said information to implement this POA.

TO: All persons, let it be known that the Delegate,

Delegate →			
	Full Legal Name:		Signature:
	Today's Date:		

In the presence of a Notary, the Delegate has accepted the Appointment for the DOAP as the acting Subservient Agent. The Delegate understands the full import and meaning of this Appointment. The Delegate affirms the following in the Notary's presence: (**01**) The Delegate is at least eighteen (**18**) years or older. (**02**) The Delegate is of sound and disposing mind (emotionally and mentally competent). (**03**) The Delegate has the capacity with full memory or necessary mental faculties to understand and comprehend these actions. (**04**) The Delegate willfully and voluntarily executes this Appointment. The Delegate declares that this paragraph is true and correct under the Penalty of Perjury.

References to DOAP

The DOAP granting the Delegate's authority, rights, and powers has the following date of execution:

Month of: ______ **Day of:** _______ **Year of:** ______ ← **Date of execution of the DOAP**

A formal recording/filing (optional) of a true copy of the DOAP is with the following:

Public Records of:				
	Location's Name:		Docket #	
	Location's Address:		Page #	

UNDER THE LAWS OF → STATE: ____________________, COUNTY: ____________

Before the Notary Public (the undersigned authority) comes forth, the Delegate, with a sound/disposed mind, is eighteen (**18**) years or older. The Delegate acknowledges having willfully and voluntarily dated and signed this Appointment (or ask/direct for such actions to occur) stated above in the Notary Public's presence. Furthermore, the Notary Public states that the Delegate has provided a Government Issue identification card with a facial picture to prove identity. The Notary Public declares under the Penalty of Perjury that this paragraph is true and correct.

DIRECTION FOR NOTARY PUBLIC: The Notary Public shall verify the Delegate's Identity with a Government Issue Picture I.D. The Notary Public must see the following: (**01**) True Original Copy of POA and DOAP and (**02**) Delegate Designation on the POA and DOAP. If the Delegate signs this Appointment but not in the presence of the Notary Public, then the Notary Public will not notarize or sign this Appointment.

Notary Public →				
	Full Legal Name:		Signature & Seal :	
	Location Name:			
	Address:		Commission Number:	
	Phone Number:			
	Today's Date:		Commission Expires:	

Acknowledgment of Resignation by Delegate

This page is intentionally blank so that reproduction (photocopy or print) of this page may occur by the Delegate.

ACKNOWLEDGMENT OF RESIGNATION BY DELEGATE

A: For purposes of brevity and consistency, the following abbreviation shall occur: ______ shall be "**POA**," Delegation of Agent's Power shall be "**DOAP**," Subservient Agent shall be "**Delegate**," and Acknowledgment of Resignation by Delegate shall be "**Resignation**."

B: The Principal requests that the acting Delegate completes this Resignation; this Resignation is optional (may be required) but highly recommended.

C: The Delegate agrees to keep all information (health, financial, relationship, or other personal matters) confidential and shall not disclose information to outsiders unless those individuals are relevant Third Parties that require said information to implement this POA.

TO: All persons, let it be known that the Delegate,

Delegate →		
Full Legal Name:		**Signature:**
Today's Date:		

The Delegate understands the full import and meaning of this Resignation. The Delegate affirms the following in the Notary's presence: (**01**) The Delegate is at least eighteen (**18**) years or older. (**02**) The Delegate is of sound and disposing mind (emotionally and mentally competent). (**03**) The Delegate has the capacity with full memory or necessary mental faculties to understand and comprehend these actions. (**04**) The Delegate willfully and voluntarily executes this Resignation. The Delegate declares that this paragraph is true and correct under the Penalty of Perjury.

Delegate's reason for Resignation

Directions: Please check "✓" the block and then initial the line "🖉" next to the selection below that best fits the Delegate situation; select only (**01**) one option for each option is mutually exclusive to each other.

☐ Check ↑	____ Initial ↑	**Resign**	☐ Check ↑	____ Initial ↑	**Refuses**	☐ Check ↑	____ Initial ↑	**Unable**

In the presence of a Notary, the Delegate acknowledges their resignation status (stated above) as to their inability to act for the Principal; thus, the Delegate relinquishes their role and all rights thereof as the Delegate in reference to the POA (stated below). The Delegate declares that this paragraph is true and correct under the Penalty of Perjury.

References to DOAP

The DOAP from which the Delegate is resigning has the following date of execution:

Month of: ______ **Day of:** ______ **Year of:** ______ ← **Date of execution of the DOAP**

A formal recording/filing (optional) of a true copy of the DOAP is with the following:

Public Records of:				
	Location's Name:		**Docket #**	
	Location's Address:		**Page #**	

UNDER THE LAWS OF ➔ STATE: ____________, COUNTY: ____________

Before the Notary Public (the undersigned authority) comes forth, the Delegate, with a sound/disposed mind, is eighteen (**18**) years or older. The Delegate acknowledges having willfully and voluntarily dated and signed this Resignation (or ask/direct for such actions to occur) stated above in the Notary Public's presence. Furthermore, the Notary Public states that the Delegate has provided a Government Issue identification card with a facial picture to prove identity. The Notary Public declares under the Penalty of Perjury that this paragraph is true and correct.

DIRECTION FOR NOTARY PUBLIC: The Notary Public shall verify the Delegate's Identity with a Government Issue Picture I.D. If the Delegate signs this Appointment but not in the presence of the Notary Public, then the Notary Public will not notarize or sign this Appointment.

Notary Public →			
Full Legal Name:		**Signature & Seal :**	
Location Name:			
Address:			
Phone Number:		**Commission Number:**	
Today's Date:		**Commission Expires:**	

CHAPTER 05

CHAPTER

05

Forms (Miscellaneous)

CHAPTER 05

Overview

CHAPTER

05

Forms (Miscellaneous)

Overview

The following documents are available if the Principal needs them; these documents are optional. However, each document can stand alone and be very useful, think of them as an administrative support document that will make the Agent's life easier.

- **Statement of Wishes** **(01 Pages Total)**
  This document is optional and not legally enforceable; however, it may provide clarification and insight into another document that the Principal may have enacted.

- **Personal Information Worksheet** **(01 Pages Total)**
  This document is optional; this document consists of the Principal's personal information, which the Agent will find helpful in carrying out the Principal wishes.

- **Notification / Contact List** **(02 Pages Total)**
  This document is optional; consider it an extensive contact list of key individuals, which the Agent should know to carry out the Principal wishes.

- **Personal Documents Locator** **(02 Pages Total)**
  This document is optional; however, it is highly advantageous (this should cut down on time and save the Agent a big headache concerning finding the document and carrying out the Principal wishes).

- **Legal Documents Locator** **(03 Pages Total)**
  This document is optional; however, it is highly advantageous (this should cut down on time and save the Agent a big headache concerning finding the document and carrying out the Principal wishes).

Statement of Wishes

STATEMENT OF WISHES

The Principal (stated below), do at this moment set forth particular wishes/requests regarding this Legal Document.

Principal →

Full Legal Name:			
Current Address:			
Phone Number:		**E-mail:**	
Residence:	**County:**		**State :**

Legal Document: ______________________________

To the personal representatives, heirs, family, friends, and other individuals, the Principal understands that these wishes/requests are advisory only and not mandatory. The Principal wishes/requests are as follows:

Principal →

Full Legal Name:		**Signature:**
Today's Date:		

Personal Information Worksheet

PERSONAL INFORMATION WORKSHEET

The Principal (stated below) has provided the following personal information regarding the Legal Document.

Legal Document: ______________________________

PERSONAL INFORMATION (The Principal)

DOB = Date of Birth
DOD = Date of Death

Full Legal Name:				DOB:	
Phone Number:		E-mail:			
Current Address / Residence:					
Mailing Address (if different):					
Social Security Number:		Medicare Number:			
Current Occupation / Vocation:					
Military Information					
Armed Forces (Military Branch):		Last Unit / Division:			
Date & Location of Discharge:		Type of Discharge:			
Children / Wards Information					
Parental Information					
Father's Full Name:		DOB:		DOD:	
Mother's Full Maiden Name:		DOB:		DOD:	

PERSONAL INFORMATION (Current Spouse)

DOB = Date of Birth
DOD = Date of Death

Full Legal Name:				DOB:	
Phone Number:		E-mail:			
Current Address / Residence:					
Mailing Address (if different):					
Social Security Number:		Medicare Number:			
Current Occupation / Vocation:					
Military Information					
Armed Forces (Military Branch):		Last Unit / Division:			
Date & Location of Discharge:		Type of Discharge:			
Children / Wards Information					
Parental Information					
Father's Full Name:		DOB:		DOD:	
Mother's Full Maiden Name:		DOB:		DOD:	

PERSONAL INFORMATION (Former Spouse)

DOB = Date of Birth
DOD = Date of Death

Full Legal Name:				DOB:	
Phone Number:		E-mail:			
Current Address / Residence:					
Mailing Address (if different):					
Social Security Number:		Medicare Number:			
Current Occupation / Vocation:					
Military Information					
Armed Forces (Military Branch):		Last Unit / Division:			
Date & Location of Discharge:		Type of Discharge:			
Children / Wards Information					
Parental Information					
Father's Full Name:		DOB:		DOD:	
Mother's Full Maiden Name:		DOB:		DOD:	

Notification / Contact List

NOTIFICATION / CONTACT LIST

The Principal (stated below) has provided the following Notification / Contact List regarding the Legal Document.

Principal →

Full Legal Name:			
Current Address:			
Phone Number:		**E-mail:**	
Residence:	**County:**		**State :**

Legal Document: ______________________________

Notification List (non-relatives)

Accountant:	Name:	Location/Address:	Phone #:
Attorney:	**Name:**	**Location/Address:**	**Phone #:**
Banker:	**Name:**	**Location/Address:**	**Phone #:**
Clergyman:	**Name:**	**Location/Address:**	**Phone #:**
Executor:	**Name:**	**Location/Address:**	**Phone #:**
Funeral Director:	**Name:**	**Location/Address:**	**Phone #:**
Guardian:	**Name:**	**Location/Address:**	**Phone #:**
Insurance Agent:	**Name:**	**Location/Address:**	**Phone #:**
Insurance Underwriter:	**Name:**	**Location/Address:**	**Phone #:**

Today's Date: ____________ **Initial of Principal:** ____________

Notification List (relatives)

Name:	Location/Address:	Phone #:	Relationship:

Today's Date: ______________ Initial of Principal: ______________

This page is intentionally left blank

Personal Documents Locator

PERSONAL DOCUMENTS LOCATOR

The Principal (stated below) has provided the following Personal Documents Locator regarding the Legal Document.

Principal →

Full Legal Name:	
Current Address:	
Phone Number:	**E-mail:**
Residence:	**County:** **State :**

Legal Document: ______________________________

Insurance Documents:	Location of Document:	Notes:
Birth Certificate:	**Location of Document:**	**Notes:**
Deeds and Proof of Ownership:	**Location of Document:**	**Notes:**
Marriage License or Certificate:	**Location of Document:**	**Notes:**
Social Security Cards:	**Location of Document:**	**Notes:**
Military Records:	**Location of Document:**	**Notes:**
Pensions / Annuities:	**Location of Document:**	**Notes/Dates:**
Warranties:	**Location of Document:**	**Notes:**

Today's Date: ____________ **Initial of Principal:** ____________

Mortgage Documents:	Location of Document:	Notes:
Bank Documents:	**Location of Document:**	**Notes:**
Passport(s):	**Location of Document:**	**Notes:**
Tax Returns:	**Location of Document:**	**Notes:**
Business Papers:	**Location of Document:**	**Notes:**
Death Certificates:	**Location of Document:**	**Notes:**
Medical Records:	**Location of Document:**	**Notes:**
USB Drives / Portable Hard Drives:	**Location of Document:**	**Notes:**
Password & Account Info:	**Location of Document:**	**Notes:**

Today's Date: ______________ **Initial of Principal:** ______________

This page is intentionally left blank

Legal Documents Locator

LEGAL DOCUMENTS LOCATOR

The Principal (stated below) has provided the following Legal Documents Locator regarding the Legal Document.

Principal →

Full Legal Name:			
Current Address:			
Phone Number:		**E-mail:**	
Residence:	**County:**		**State :**

Legal Document: ______________________________

Affidavit (Health State):	Location of Document:	Execution Date:
Simple Power of Attorney	**Location of Document:**	**Execution Date**
Complex Power of Attorney	**Location of Document:**	**Execution Date**
Special Power of Attorney (Taxes, Vehicles):	**Location of Document:**	**Execution Date:**
Durable Power of Attorney	**Location of Document:**	**Execution Date:**

Today's Date: ______________ **Initial of Principal:** ______________

Declaration of Guardian / Conservator:	Location of Document:	Execution Date:

Advance Medical Health Directive:	Location of Document:	Execution Date:

Advance Mental Health Directive:	Location of Document:	Execution Date:

Durable Health Care Power of Attorney:	Location of Document:	Execution Date:

Do Not Resuscitate Advance Directive:	Location of Document:	Execution Date:

Declaration of Organ & Tissue Donation:	Location of Document:	Execution Date:

Today's Date: ______________ **Initial of Principal:** ______________

Cohabitation Agreement:	Location of Document:	Execution Date:

Prenuptial / Postnuptial Agreement:	Location of Document:	Execution Date:

Separation Agreements:	Location of Document:	Execution Date:

Parenting Plan / Visitation Agreement:	Location of Document:	Execution Date:

Divorce Decree:	Location of Document:	Execution Date:

Last Will and Testaments / Codicil:	Location of Document:	Execution Date:

Trusts Agreements	Location of Document:	Execution Date:

Court Orders:	Location of Document:	Execution Date:

Revocation:	Location of Document:	Execution Date:

Today's Date: ______________ **Initial of Principal:** ______________

CHAPTER 06

CHAPTER

06

Forms (Recommended)

CHAPTER 06

Overview

CHAPTER

06

Forms (Recommended)

Overview

The following documents are available if the Principal needs them; these documents are optional. However, each document can stand alone and be very useful, think of them as an administrative support document that will make the Agent's life easier.

- **Affidavit of Principal's Health State** **(03 Pages Total)**
  The Affidavit of Principal's Health State is a proactive legal document. The Principal has sought a Health Professional to ascertain and verify that the Principal is competent, has the capacity, and functions socially. Implementation of this legal document typically occurs to prevent any future legal challenges; this supporting document is optional but highly recommended.

- **Assets & Liabilities Worksheet** **(08 Pages Total)**
  This optional supporting document is an easy, straightforward balance sheet (Asset minus Liabilities) that will help save the Agent time, effort, and energy.

- **Self – Proving Affidavit** **(01 Page Total)**
  The Self-Proving Affidavit is an optional document that accompanies a POA and verifies its validity. The affidavit may help speed up the legal process and potentially save on legal fees.

Affidavit of Principal's Health State

This page is intentionally blank so the Health Professional may reproduce (photocopy or print) it.

AFFIDAVIT OF PRINCIPAL'S HEALTH STATE

For purposes of brevity and consistency, the following acronym/abbreviation shall occur: Affidavit of Principal's Health State shall be "**Affidavit**," and Medical/Mental Health Professional (licensed physician, licensed psychologist, licensed psychiatrist) shall be "**Health Professional**."

TO: All persons, let it be known that the Health Professional,

Health Professional →

Full Legal Name:

Current Address:

Phone Number: **Email:**

Residence: **County:** **State:**

Having now duly sworn, deposes, and says that the:

Principal →

Full Legal Name:

Current Address:

Phone Number: **Email:**

Residence: **County:** **State:**

In the presence of a Health Professional, the Principal states the following: **(1)** The Principal is at least eighteen **(18)** years or older. **(2)** The Principal requested this Affidavit regarding their Health State status. **(3)** The Principal willfully and voluntarily asks for this evaluation to determine their Health State status for this Affidavit.

Health Professional Statements

DIRECTIONS: The Health Professional must **place "Y" for Yes or "N" for No in the box and initial "✐" the line to all that is applicable** in the corresponding empty box space below that the Health Professional has performed. For the comment box, please type any relevant information about the Principal.

"Y" or "N" Here ↑ | Initial Here ↑ | **Personally Examine** | The Health Professional has personally examined/interviewed the Principal to determine their health state status on the following: Date: ______ Time: ______

"Y" or "N" Here ↑ | Initial Here ↑ | **Review Health Records** | The Health Professional has reviewed the relevant medical/mental health history, if available, and made it known to the Health Professional.

"Y" or "N" Here ↑ | Initial Here ↑ | **Proof of Identity** | The Health Professional has reviewed and verified the Principal's identity with a government-issued identification card with a facial picture.

The history of the Health Professional involvement with the Principal is the following:

Specify in Detail

Preferably Type or Legible writing in Ink

Initial of Notary Public: ______ **Initial of Health Professional:** ______

Specify in Detail

The Health Professional has performed or ordered the following tests /examinations:

The Principal is unable to perform the following functions (if Healthy type N/A):

Describe the Principal's health condition (incapacity, incompetency, or function non-socially). Provide the date and duration of any illness and the approximate full or partial recovery date.

Preferably Type or Legible writing in Ink

Health Professional Evaluations

DIRECTIONS: The Health Professional must **place "Y" for Yes or "N" for No in the box and initial "✐" the line to all that is applicable** in the corresponding empty box space below. There are (**04**) Options available. However, **Healthy** is mutually exclusive to **Incapacitated, Incompetent, and Function Non-Socially**.

In the opinion of the Health Professional, based on tests, examinations, or interviews, the Principal is the following:

"Y" or "N" Here ↑ Initial Here ↑

Place "Y" for Yes or "N" for No in the box and initial "✐" the line if the Principal is the following:

Incapacitated

DESCRIPTION: By designating "Y" for Yes, the Health Professional has determined, under the penalty of perjury, that the Principal is **Incapacitated** and has one or more of the following conditions: (**01**) The Principal cannot make, participate, or communicate a decision regarding their health care. (**02**) The Principal cannot manage the following: their care, property, or financial affairs. When trying to conceptualize what an incapacitated individual can do, think of an individual unable to control their motor movement and needing help to do regular tasks. Examples include (but are not limited to) the following: Amyotrophic Lateral Sclerosis (ALS), Primary Lateral Sclerosis (PLS), Progressive Bulbar Palsy (PBP), Progressive Muscular Atrophy (PMA), Pseudobulbar Palsy, and Parkinson's disease.

"Y" or "N" Here ↑ Initial Here ↑

Place "Y" for Yes or "N" for No in the box and initial "✐" the line if the Principal is the following:

Incompetent

DESCRIPTION: By designating "Y" for Yes, the Health Professional has determined, under the penalty of perjury, that the Principal is **Incompetent** and has one or more of the following conditions: (**01**) The Principal cannot understand and appreciate the extent, nature, and probable consequences of a proposed medical and mental health decision that may or may not have life-sustaining implications. (**02**) The Principal cannot make an informed, intelligent decision in a reasonable amount of time. (**03**) The Principal cannot communicate a coherent decision no matter how simple the communication process is. (**04**) The Principal cannot rationally evaluate the risks and benefits of a proposed medical and mental health decision compared to the risks and benefits of alternatives. Examples include (but are not limited to) the following: Alzheimer's disease, Huntington's disease, Schizophrenia, Psychotic Disorder, and Severe Dementia. **Please Note:** An individual with a mental illness, advanced age, or developmental disability does not automatically imply or constitute a lack of decisional capacity.

Initial of Notary Public: ____________ **Initial of Health Professional:** ____________

Function Non-Socially

Place "Y" for Yes or "N" for No in the box and initial "✐" the line if the Principal is the following:

"Y" or "N" Here ↑ Initial Here ↑

DESCRIPTION: By designating "Y" for Yes, the Health Professional has determined, under the penalty of perjury, that the Principal **Function Non-Socially**, and cannot demonstrate one or more of the following: to recognize people, communicate with people, and interact with people in a meaningful way.

Healthy

Place "Y" for Yes or "N" for No in the box and initial "✐" the line if the Principal is the following:

"Y" or "N" Here ↑ Initial Here ↑

DESCRIPTION: By designating "Y" for Yes, the Health Professional has determined, under the penalty of perjury, that the Principal is **Healthy** and exhibits capacity with complete mental competence, thus fully capable of independent thought and actions, and functions socially.

Consult Local or State Law to determine Signature and Notary Requirements for the Affidavit (for said requirements may be less strict); however, prudence suggests having the Health Professional's signature notarized.

The Health Professional, having noted the existence of this Affidavit, personally placed a copy in the Principal's permanent medical/ mental health records. The Health Professional affirms their impartiality and understands with full knowledge that utilization of this Affidavit shall occur in acceptance of execution and delivery of other pertinent legal documents. The Health Professional declares this paragraph is true and correct under the Penalty of Perjury.

Please Note: Some states allow Nurse practitioners and Physician Assistants the authority to sign and issue on behalf of the Health Professional regarding an Affidavit.

Health Professional →

Full Legal Name:		**Signature:** ✐	
Today's Date:			
Board Certification:		**License # & State:**	
Occupation / Specialty:		**License Expires:**	

UNDER THE LAWS OF →

COUNTY: ____________________

STATE: ____________________

Before the Notary Public (the undersigned authority) comes forth, the Health Professional, with a sound/disposed mind, is eighteen (**18**) years or older. The Health Professional acknowledges having willfully and voluntarily dated and signed this Affidavit (or asked/directed for such actions to occur) stated above in the Notary Public presence. Furthermore, the Notary Public states that the Health Professional has provided a Government Issue identification card with a facial picture to prove identity. The Notary Public declares under the Penalty of Perjury that this paragraph is true and correct.

DIRECTION FOR NOTARY PUBLIC: The Notary Public shall verify the Health Professional's Identity with a Government Issue Picture I.D. If the Health Professional signs this Affidavit but not in the presence of the Notary Public, then the Notary Public will not notarize or sign this Affidavit.

Notary Public →

Full Name:		**Signature & Seal:** ✐	
Location:			
Address:			
Phone #:		**I.D. Number:**	
Date:		**Commission Expires:**	

Initial of Notary Public: ____________ **Initial of Health Professional:** ____________

Assets & Liabilities Worksheet

ASSETS & LIABILITIES WORKSHEET

The Assets & Liability Worksheet shall be attached to the following Legal Document:

The Assets & Liability Worksheet relates to the following individual as stated below:

Principal →

Full Legal Name:
Current Address:
Phone Number: E-mail:
Residence: County: State :

I. ASSETS (what the Principal owns)

A. LIQUID ASSETS (Easily convertible assets that can become cash, for example, money-market funds, Treasury Bills, and bank deposit.)

1. Cash (dividends, et cetera)

Description (Date & Title)	[1]Ownership	[2]Net Value $

2. Savings and Checking Accounts

Name/Location of Financial Intuition	Type	Account #	[1]Ownership	[2]Net Value $

3. Money Market Accounts

Name/Location of Financial Intuition	Interest / Dividends	Account #	[1]Ownership	[2]Net Value $

[1]**Ownership:** Who owns the property, and how is the property title (joint tenancy, community property, et cetera.)? [2]**Net Value:** The amount remaining after certain deductions (debts) viewed it as the Principals "take away" amount. [3]**Net Amount Owed:** The amount of liability remaining after all accounted monetary payments, think of it as "what the Principal still owes" amount.

Today's Date: ______________ **Initial of Principal:** ______________

LIQUID ASSETS (CONTINUED)

4. Certificates of Deposit

Name/Location of Financial Intuition	Interest / Dividends	Account #	[1]Ownership	[2]Net Value $

5. Mutual Funds

Name/Location of Financial Intuition	Interest / Dividends	Account #	[1]Ownership	[2]Net Value $

6. Trust Income / Estates Income

Description	Interest / Dividends	[2]Net Value $

[1]**Ownership:** Who owns the property, and how is the property title (joint tenancy, community property, et cetera.)? [2]**Net Value:** The amount remaining after certain deductions (debts) viewed it as the Principals "take away" amount. [3]**Net Amount Owed:** The amount of liability remaining after all accounted monetary payments, think of it as "what the Principal still owes" amount.

Today's Date: ______________ **Initial of Principal:** ______________

B. OTHER PERSONAL PROPERTY

1. Listed (Private Corporation) Stocks and Bonds

Description/Name of Stock or Bond	[1]Ownership	# of shares	Certificate #	[2]Net Value $

2. Unlisted Stocks and Bonds

Description/Name of Stock or Bond	[1]Ownership	# of shares	Certificate #	[2]Net Value $

3. Government Bonds

Description of Bond	[1]Ownership	Certificate #	[2]Net Value $

4. Automobiles, Planes, Boats, Recreational Vehicles, etc.

Description (Year, Make, Model, Vin #, Reg #, or ID #)	[1]Ownership	[2]Net Value $

[1]**Ownership:** Who owns the property, and how is the property title (joint tenancy, community property, et cetera.)? [2]**Net Value:** The amount remaining after certain deductions (debts) viewed it as the Principals "take away" amount. [3]**Net Amount Owed:** The amount of liability remaining after all accounted monetary payments, think of it as "what the Principal still owes" amount.

Today's Date: ____________ **Initial of Principal:** ____________

OTHER PERSONAL PROPERTY (CONTINUED)

5. Valuable Livestock/Animals

Description (Date & Title)	²Net Value $

6. Debt Receivables, personal loan, Etc.

Description (Date & Title)	²Net Value $

7. Vested Interest in a Profit-Sharing Plan, Stock Options, Etc.

Description (Date & Title)	Beneficiary (if any)	¹Ownership	²Net Value $

8. Vested Interest in a Retirement Plans, Pensions, Death Benefits, or Annuities.

Description (Date & Title)	Beneficiary (if any)	¹Ownership	²Net Value $

[1]**Ownership:** Who owns the property, and how is the property title (joint tenancy, community property, et cetera.)? [2]**Net Value:** The amount remaining after certain deductions (debts) viewed it as the Principals "take away" amount. [3]**Net Amount Owed:** The amount of liability remaining after all accounted monetary payments, think of it as "what the Principal still owes" amount.

Today's Date: ____________ **Initial of Principal:** ____________

OTHER PERSONAL PROPERTY (CONTINUED)

9. Life Insurance

Insurance Company	Policy #	Beneficiary	[2]Net Value $

10. Miscellaneous: (Any personal property not listed above, examples include, but not limited, to the following: Tools, Equipment, Artwork, Collectibles, antiques, jewelry, household goods, et cetera)

Description (Date & Title)	Type	[2]Net Value $

C. BUSINESS PERSONAL PROPERTY

1. Patents, Copyrights, Trademarks, and Royalties

Description (Date & Title)	Type	[2]Net Value $

[1]**Ownership:** Who owns the property, and how is the property title (joint tenancy, community property, et cetera.)? [2]**Net Value:** The amount remaining after certain deductions (debts) viewed it as the Principals "take away" amount. [3]**Net Amount Owed:** The amount of liability remaining after all accounted monetary payments, think of it as "what the Principal still owes" amount.

Today's Date: ____________ **Initial of Principal:** ____________

BUSINESS PERSONAL PROPERTY (CONTINUED)

2. Business Interest: (Sole Proprietorship, Partnerships, Limited Partnership, Limited Liability Corporation, Subchapter S Corporation, Corporation, et cetera)

Name of Business	Type	Ownership Interest %	[2]Net Value $

3. Miscellaneous Receivables: (example includes, but not limited, to the following: (01) mortgages, deeds of trust, or promissory notes held by the Principal. (02) Rental income that is payable and due to the Principal. (03) Deferred Commissions, Other Non-Real Estates Contracts such as payments due for professional or personal services, or property sold.)

Description (Date & Title)	Type	[2]Net Value $

D. REAL ESTATE

1. Residential (may also include Real Estate Contracts, Rental Income minus Expense)

Location (and Legal Description if Known)	[1]Ownership	Mortgage Amount	[2]Net Value $ (Of Mortgage)

[1]**Ownership:** Who owns the property, and how is the property title (joint tenancy, community property, et cetera.)? [2]**Net Value:** The amount remaining after certain deductions (debts) viewed it as the Principals "take away" amount. [3]**Net Amount Owed:** The amount of liability remaining after all accounted monetary payments, think of it as "what the Principal still owes" amount.

Today's Date: ______________ **Initial of Principal:** ______________

REAL ESTATE (CONTINUED)

2. Commercial (may also include Real Estate Contracts, Rental Income minus Expense)

Location (and Legal Description if Known)	[1]Ownership	Mortgage Amount	[2]Net Value $ (Of Mortgage)

E. TOTAL NET VALUE OF ALL PRINCIPAL'S ASSETS: (Add up Total "Net Value" of Section I.)	$

II. LIABILITIES (what the Principal owes)

Keep in mind that much of the calculation concerning the Principal obligations (debt) has already occurred in Section I. Since the calculation of the Principal worth is in "net value," this means the Principal has previously taken into account such things as mortgages, business debts, and other financial obligations. Therefore, the Principal needs only list below those debts, and other obligations owed that the Principal has not covered.

A. PERSONAL PROPERTY DEBTS

1. Personal Loans (banks, major credit cards, et cetera)

Lender / Creditor	Type	Collateral / Security	Interest Rate	[3]Net Amount Owed $

[1]**Ownership:** Who owns the property, and how is the property title (joint tenancy, community property, et cetera.)? [2]**Net Value:** The amount remaining after certain deductions (debts) viewed it as the Principals "take away" amount. [3]**Net Amount Owed:** The amount of liability remaining after all accounted monetary payments, think of it as "what the Principal still owes" amount.

Today's Date: ______________ **Initial of Principal:** ____________

PERSONAL PROPERTY DEBTS (CONTINUED)

2. Other Personal Services (Health Insurance Payment, Dental Insurance Payment, Car Insurance Payment, House Insurance Payments, Life Insurance Payments)

Description (Date & Title)	Type	[3]Net Amount Owed $

B. TAXES (Federal, State, Local, FICA, Self-Employment, Mandatory Union Dues)

(Include only taxes past and currently due; this will not include taxes due in the future or estimated taxes)

Description (Date & Title)	Type	[3]Net Amount Owed $

C. ANY OTHER LIABILITIES

(Legal Judgments Accrued Child Support Arrearage, Court Order, Contractual Child Support, Spousal Support, et cetera)

Description (Date & Title)	Type	[3]Net Amount Owed $

D. TOTAL LIABILITIES: (Excluding those liabilities already deducted in section I.)	$

III. NET WORTH

(Subtract assets (from Section I. E) from liabilities (Section II. D):	$

[1]**Ownership:** Who owns the property, and how is the property title (joint tenancy, community property, et cetera.)? [2]**Net Value:** The amount remaining after certain deductions (debts) viewed it as the Principals "take away" amount. [3]**Net Amount Owed:** The amount of liability remaining after all accounted monetary payments, think of it as "what the Principal still owes" amount.

Today's Date: ____________ **Initial of Principal:** ____________

This page is intentionally left blank

Self – Proving Affidavit

This page is intentionally blank so that Witnesses may reproduce (photocopy or print) it.

SELF-PROVING AFFIDAVIT

I, the Principal (as stated below), have signed this Power of Attorney (POA) with an execution date (as stated below):

Title of POA: ______________________ **Execution Date:** __________

I, the Principal (as stated below), being duly sworn, have subscribed, published, and declared to the undersigned authority that I, the Principal, have signed and executed the POA (as stated above). I, the Principal, attest to the following on the Execution Date (as stated above): (**01**) I am at least eighteen (**18**) years or older. (**02**) I am of sound and disposing mind (emotionally and mentally competent). (**03**) I am not suffering from constraint, duress, fraud, or undue influence. (**04**) I acknowledge having willfully and voluntarily dated and signed the POA (as stated above) or asked/directed for such actions to occur. I make this **Affidavit** by subscribing/providing my Legal Name, Today's Date, and Signature below.

Principal →		
Name:		Signature:
Date:		

In the joint presence of each other, we, the subscribing Witnesses (as stated below), duly sworn and declared to the undersigned authority that we witnessed the execution of the POA (as stated above). We witnessed the Principal (as stated above) subscribe, publish, and declare the POA (as stated above) to be the Principal's POA in our presence. We witnessed the appointment of Fiduciaries to perform according to the terms of the POA (as stated above), which may include the ability to act when the Principal is **incapacitated, incompetent, or functioning non-socially.** We attest that in the Principal's presence and at the Principal's request, we, the Witnesses, in joint presence of each other, subscribed to the POA (as stated above) on the Execution Date (as stated above). Furthermore, we, the Witnesses, state that the Principal was the following on the Execution Date (as stated above): (**01**) The Principal is at least eighteen (**18**) years or older. (**02**) The Principal is of sound and disposing mind (emotionally and mentally competent). (**03**) The Principal is not suffering from constraint, duress, fraud, or undue influence. (**04**) The Principal acknowledges having willfully and voluntarily dated and signed the POA (as stated above) or asked/directed for such actions to occur. We, the Witnesses, make this **Affidavit** at the Prinicipal's request by subscribing/providing our Legal Name, Occupation, Contact Information, Today's Date, and Signature below.

1st Witness →		
Name:		Signature:
Address:		
Phone #:		**Date:**
Occupation:		

2nd Witness →		
Name:		Signature:
Address:		
Phone #:		**Date:**
Occupation:		

UNDER THE LAWS OF → **COUNTY:** ______________________

STATE: ______________________

Before the Notary Public (the undersigned authority) comes forth, the Principal and the Witnesses, with a sound/disposed mind, are eighteen (**18**) years or older. The Principal and Witnesses subscribed, swore, and acknowledged having willfully and voluntarily dated and signed this **Affidavit** (or asked/directed for such actions to occur) in the Notary Public presence. Furthermore, the Notary Public states that the Principal and Witnesses have provided a Government Issue identification card with a facial picture to prove identity. The Notary Public declares under the Penalty of Perjury that this paragraph is true and correct.

Notary Public →		
Full Name:		**Signature & Seal:**
Location:		
Address:		
Phone #:		**I.D. Number:**
Date:		**Commission Expires:**

CHAPTER 07

CHAPTER

07

Appendices & Glossary

CHAPTER 07

Overview

CHAPTER

07

Appendices & Glossary

Overview

The following documents are available if the Principal needs them; these documents may be a requirement. However, each document can stand alone and be very useful, think of them as an administrative support document.

- **Appendix A:**
  Insurance Suggestions & Resource Guide **(03 Pages Total)**
  Consider it a Fiduciary Guide to Insurance with suggestions and insights to help maximize value and reduce information overload.

- **Appendix B:**
  Directions for Prudent & Safe Investing **(04 Pages Total)**
  Consider it a Fiduciary Guide to Prudent and Safe Investing with clear instructions and a built-in investment philosophy layout that help the fiduciary stay away from the money-sucking minefields and grow wealth safely and securely.

- **Appendix C:**
  Attorney Suggestions & Resource Guide **(02 Pages Total)**
  Consider it a Fiduciary Guide to hiring and working with an Attorney with suggestions and insights to help minimize expenses and increase productivity in a Client/Attorney relationship.

- **Appendix D:**
  Steps for Credit Repair & Statute of Limitations **(03 Pages Total)**
  Consider it a Helpful Guide to repairing or establishing Credit along with a basic overview of creditor law and associated statute of limitations.

- **Glossary:** **(08 Pages Total)**
  Consider it an informational source that includes medical, financial, business, and legal terminology.

Insurance Suggestions & Resource Guide

Insurance Suggestions & Resource Guide

Suggestions for Insurance in General:

- The following is for the Principal/Agent convenience when shopping for insurance: QuickQuote: **www.quickquote.com**; SelectQuote: **www.selectquote.com**; Insurance Quote Service: **www.iquote.com**; MasterQuote: **www.masterquote.com**; Term4Sale: **www.term4sale.com**; Insure: **www.insure.com;** Insurance: **www.insurance.com;** NetQuote: **www.netquote.com**; and Direct Insurance Service.
- Upon selecting an Insurance Provider, consider comparing the insurance to the following rating agencies: Weiss Ratings (Weiss Research): **www.weissratings.com**; A.M. Best (Best Insurance Reports): **www.ambest.com**; Moody's Investors Service: **www.moody.com**; and Standard and Poor's: **www.standardandpoors.com**. The Insurance Provider shall have a rating of "A" (or its equivalent) or above among all rating agencies. Furthermore, it must have maintained that rating history for twenty (**20**) years or more.
- Ask the Insurer if a direct-sales policy is possible; this way, the Principal/Agent eliminates the intermediary and thus lowers the insurance premiums while maintaining all the benefits. If the Principal/Agent must pursue insurance coverage through an insurance representative, consider an Independent Representative (individual selling policies from multiple insurers).
- Insurance is primarily subject to ever-changing state laws. If the Principal/Agent has any questions, seek the advice of a competent, licensed Insurance Representative or an Attorney specializing in insurance law.

Suggestions for Life Insurance:

- When determining the amount of life insurance coverage that the Principal (Insured) will need, consider the following: the primary purpose of life insurance is to provide a lump-sum payment that replaces the Insured income if a person dies unexpectedly or prematurely. The amount of insurance coverage needed is subjective and varies from individual to individual; remember the primary purpose of life insurance before deriving one's calculations.
- When selecting a life insurance policy, the Principal/Agent should buy **term life**. Why buy whole, universal, or variable when the Principal/Agent can invest the money and get a better return versus the payout by the life insurance company? **Please Note:** sometimes mathematics or statistics works out that group (if eligible), single-premium, first-to-die, or whole life (**very rarely**) may be a better option.
- Insurance that has a "cash value" component (savings account) provides the following average rates of returns after all fees: (**01**) Whole Life Insurance **1.2%**, (**02**) Universal Life Insurance **4.2%**, and (**03**) Index Universal Life Insurance **7.2%**.
- Insurance with an "investing" component provides the following average rates of returns after all fees: (01) Variable Universal Life Insurance 7% and (**02)** Variable Life Insurance **7.3%**.
- When the Principal (Insured) dies, the beneficiary will only get the policy's face amount, but the "cash value" goes to the Insurance Company, not the beneficiary. Furthermore, if the Principal (Insured) were to "borrow" the cash value, the Principal would have to pay an interest/fee on the money. Since the Insurance Company is loaning the money back to the Principal (Insured), that was lent generously to the Insurance Company for safekeeping.
- Using the power of compound interest, consider investing in a High Growth Index Mutual Fund with a low expense ratio, preferably within a Roth IRA. The advantages are as follows: (**01**) The Principal (Insured) always maintains control. (**02**) The Principal (Insured) will achieve a greater rate of return on investment (8% to 12% after fees) over a long-time horizon. (**03**) The Principal (Insured) will never surrender the "cash value" to the Insurance Company. (**04**) The beneficiary shall receive the investment if death occurs. (**05**) No interest/fee occurs if the Principal (Insured) needs to cash some or all of the investment early. "Never buy life insurance as an investment; the math [will] never [ever] work [in one's favor]." ~ Dave Ramsey
- The payment option for the term life insurance shall be as follows: "Lump Sum."
- Consider purchasing fixed premium fixed terms "Level" Insurance; however, annual renewal policies shall be permissible – read carefully what the renewal rights are. Depending on the insured's age, if age forty (**40**) years or older, consider a policy that automatically renews without a medical examination (thus justifying the additional increase in premiums).
- The term life insurance length should be in five (**05**) to ten (**10**) year intervals if the Principal (Insured) is under the age of forty (**40**), if over the age of forty (**40**), then considers a twenty-year term policy.
- Consider a Layered Insurance Policy or a Decreasing Term Policy if the Principal (Insured) wants top-heavy insurance coverage at a younger age and lesser coverage at an older age. This insurance coverage method dovetails very nicely with the Theory of Decreasing Responsibility.

Principal: ______

- Do not name the Principal's Estate as the life insurance policy's **beneficiary**; by doing so, the life insurance proceeds will become taxable, delays will develop, and the possibility of a reduction in payout - due to debt and creditors. The Principal will benefit significantly by naming a competent adult beneficiary; if that is not an option, it is best to establish a trust and name it the beneficiary. If the Principal is married, the Principal can also name their spouse as the beneficiary; there will be no estate or federal tax on those proceeds.
- The Principal should consider establishing a living trust as the insurance policy's beneficiary if the insurance policy proceeds to benefit a minor child; this will avoid court-appointed property guardianship, attorney's fees, court proceedings, and court supervision.
- The Principal can establish a method to impose adult management on the proceeds using a Child's Trust Arrangement or UTMA custodianship in the trust document.

Suggestions for Disability Insurance:

- If possible, buy disability insurance from the Principal's employer (usually cheaper); however, the benefits are taxable. If the Principal pays for disability insurance, the benefits are tax-free.
- Calculations for disability insurance coverage quotes are in dollars per month, which the Principal will receive if disabled. Thus, consider getting a policy that reflects the Principal monthly take-home pay; for example, the Principal makes $2,500 after monthly taxes; therefore, seek a policy that provides $2,500 in benefits.
- Disability coverage duration should be the Principal natural retirement age (usually 65 through 67) minus the Principal current age; if the Principal is financially secure, then the duration of coverage could be even less. Remember, the purpose of Disability Insurance is to replace income if the Principal cannot work.
- The deductible is the waiting period (Lag Time) from filing the claim due to disability to collecting the financial benefits. The longer the duration for Lag Time, the cheaper the insurance; thus, consider a waiting period of ninety (**90**) days to (**06**) six months if financially able.
- Ensure the Principal/Agent reads the fine print of the definition of disability and occupation. Some policies will only pay out if the Principal cannot perform a job, not necessarily the Principal's current occupation. If the Principal is in a high-income profession or specialized occupation, consider buying an Own-Occupation Disability Policy. These are more expensive but may be well worth the expense.
- Always get a Non-Cancelable, Guaranteed Renewable, Guaranteed Eligibility policy; this prevents policy cancellation due to poor health conditions. Otherwise, the Principal shall be required to take periodic physical exams, which may result in losing insurance coverage when the Principal (Insured) needs it most.
- Consider Residual benefits (if the premium increase is minimal); this option pays a partial benefit if the Principal has a disability that prevents working full-time.
- Always get the Cost-of-Living-Adjustments (COLA); this maintains the purchasing power of the benefits by keeping up with inflation; a four (**04**) percent COLA is worth having.
- Avoid miscellaneous options such as future insurability, additional riders, small items, and other add-on features; these options are usually unnecessary and not worth the extra premiums.
- **Statistical Facts:** (**01**) The average person is three times more likely to suffer a life-altering disability versus dying prematurely during their working years. (**02**) According to the Social Security Administration, approximately ninety (90) percent of disabling accidents and illnesses are not directly work-related.

Suggestions for Long-Term Care Insurance:

- Long-term care Insurance is most important if the Principal feels there may be a need for a home health aide or full-time nursing home care soon.
- Long-Term Care Insurance is more important for individuals with moderate income. Individuals who have too many assets to qualify for Medicaid coverage but too little to cover nursing home(s), custodial care, and other expenses (which can easily exceed $60,000 yearly).
- When applying for Medicaid, remember that qualified plans are usually exempt as an asset for Medicaid if they are in a "payout status." However, Medicaid views payments from a qualified plan as income; thus, Medicaid recipients must be careful of threshold limitations since anything above a certain amount will go to the Health Care Service Provider instead.
- Payout status can begin at 59.5 years; however, RMD (require minimum distributions) currently starts at 72 years of age (subject to change). State laws vary significantly regarding Medicaid; consult a competent licensed Attorney specializing in Estate Planning or Elderly Law for any questions or concerns.

Principal: ______

Suggestion for Final Expense (Burial) Insurance:

- Final Expense/Burial Insurance is a rip-off that preys on people's fears. Instead, the Principal is better off buying a Term-Life Insurance Policy if possible. Some policies do not require a health examination; however, the face amount is typically low ($25,000 to $50,000). Why buy Term-Life Insurance for funeral expenses? The final disposition service provider can place an assignment on the Life Insurance Policy policy, thus paying the Final Expense/Burial from the face amount of the death benefits.
- Other alternatives include establishing an emergency account and contributing at least $5,000 (for Cremation) to $15,000 (for a Traditional Funeral) to a Money Market Mutual Fund using a brokerage account.

Suggestions for Decreasing Reliance on Insurance:

- Have a credit card with an available credit limit of **$1,000 to $5,000** for very short-term liquidity. Use the fully funded emergency account to pay off the credit card balance within a month.
- Establish a fully funded emergency account that covers at least six (**06**) to twelve (**12**) months of expenses, preferably in the following accounts: (**01**) High-Yield Interest-Bearing Bank Account with the highest APY possible. (**02**) Money-Market Fund or Tax-free Money-Market Fund (depending on the individual Tax Bracket) with the highest APY possible.
- By establishing a fully funded emergency account, the Principal (Insured) decreases or potentially eliminates the need for Final Expense and Short-Term Disability insurance.
- When establishing a Money-Market Fund or Tax-free Money-Market Fund, the Principal/Agent should utilize a passive management approach with ETF and Mutual Fund with a Low Expense Ratio. The top five (**05**) best brokerage and retirement accounts are BlackRock, Vanguard, Fidelity, iShare, and American Funds.
- The need for Term Life Insurance versus Retirement Savings is inversely related. The greater the liquid assets available in a Retirement account, the lesser the need for Term Life Insurance and vice versa. Hence, the saying "Buy Term, and Invest the Rest."

Directions for Prudent & Safe Investing

Directions for Prudent & Safe Investing

Follow these rules, and the Principal's investment experience shall be better than the norm:

A. The Principal / Agent will encounter various titles such as Financial Manager, Trust Manager, Financial Advisor, Financial Planner, Broker, et cetera when investing; make sure to ask if that individual or firm is a **Fiduciary** in the legal sense. Before having business dealings, ensure that the individual or firm says "**yes**" to their fiduciary status in writing. The Fiduciary shall invest and manage assets held in a **fiduciary capacity** as a prudent (reasonable exercising care, skill, and caution) investor would, considering the purposes, terms, and distribution requirements expressed in the "**Goals and Objectives Contract**."

B. Usually, substantial unexpected financial wealth occurs in a lump sum one-time payment: Life Insurance Proceeds, Court Settlements, Lottery Winnings, and Inheritance. The Fiduciary shall hold said monetary wealth in the following financial vehicle/arrangement for a short-term period (less than one year): (**01**) High-Yield Interest-Bearing Bank Account (up to FDIC Insurance coverage limits) with the highest APY possible or a (**02**) Money-Market Fund or Tax-free Money-Market Fund (depending on the individual Tax Bracket) with the highest APY possible. If the Principal / Agent situation is complicated, seek help from a reputable CPA / Tax Attorney and an Asset Protection Lawyer. If the death of a loved one occurs, please allow for a three (**03**) to six (**06**) months grieving period to pass before making any significant financial decisions and seek a therapist if needed.

C. The investor shall seek out financial advice on a **fee-only** basis to prevent conflict of interest. Financial advice shall come from one of the following Individuals: Certified Financial Planner (**CFP**), Certified Financial Analyst (**CFA**), Chartered Financial Consultant (**ChFC**), Chartered Investment Counselor (**CIC**), or Personal Financial Specialist (**CPA/PFS**). The investor will benefit from seeking this advice within thirty (**30**) calendar days of distribution from the insurance company or other entity. The investor shall outline goals/objectives and any limitations to the Fiduciary to determine the appropriate asset allocation and achieve the investor's goals/objectives within their risk tolerance. CFP, CFA, ChFC, CIC, and CPA/PFS have some of the highest fiduciary and educational standards in the financial service industry.

D. Regarding the Equities portion of the investment portfolio, the above Fiduciary shall only engage in Strategic Asset Allocation (SAA), utilizing a Constant Mix Strategy. However, if the investment portfolio exceeds $500,000, then Global Tactical Asset Allocation (GTAA) shall be permissible for Equities concerning International and Emerging Markets.

E. The Fiduciary shall strive to use No-Load Index Funds and Exchange-Traded Funds (ETF); however, Leverage Funds and ETF utilization shall not occur. Investing in High-Dividend Stock, Preferred Stock, and Convertible Bonds shall only occur after much research and debate.

F. Due to the Fiduciary requirements, the Agent or Trustee shall not engage in the following investment/ practices: buying on margin, utilizing the Securities within the investment portfolio as collateral, buying individual stocks and bonds, and limited partnership.

G. Annuities (Fixed, Indexed, and Variable) have their place in retirement planning; however, a break-even analysis shall occur based on the following factors: Life Expectancy, Time-Horizon, Liquidity, Fees & Expenses, and available Financial Assets before purchasing an Annuity. Consider doing a simple Time Value Analysis to determine which approach will generate greater returns. For example, a 5% Annual Compound Rate of an Initial Amount of $20,000 with no additional payments: 10 years = $32.577.89; 20 years = $53,065.95; 30 years = $86.438.85; 40 years = $140,799.77; 50 years = $229, 348.00; 60 years = $373,583.72. Do not underestimate the power of compound interest over a long-term time horizon.

H. Warren Buffet's insight and advice are worth their weight in gold. Suggested reading: **Think, Act, and Invest like Warren Buffet** by **Larry E. Swedroe**.

18 Ways to Get the Best Financial Advice by Paul M. Paquette

"Trust, but verify."
~ Old Russian Proverb

01. If the Principal / Agent consults with a financial advisor, verify professional credentials such as CFP, CFA, ChFC, CIC, and CPA/PFS.

02. Look for a fee-only financial planner that charges an hourly rate. Start one's search at the CFP Board of Standards (**www.cfp.net**) or the National Association of Personal Financial Advisors (**www.napfa.org**).

03. Is there regulatory action(s) (past or present) against the financial planner? Visit **FINRA.org** and **SEC.gov** to see whether the financial planner is licensed/registered at the state securities department. Visit (**NASAA.org**) to find out if there is any history of complaints. Check the state's insurance division if the financial planner sells insurance or annuity products.

04. Never commit to handing over any money at the first meeting. Think about this financial decision and talk to others. Stop and leave immediately if the financial planner pressures the Principal / Agent into a service agreement.

Principal: ______

I. The use of Sector Funds is allowable (suggest no more than 10% of each sector category).

J. Buying Precious Metals (subsect of Commodities) as an asset class is slightly discouraged; however, if the Principal / Agent insists on holding this asset class, it shall be with the knowledge and understanding that this is not an investment. Physical purchases of precious metals shall be at an all-time three-year low, and liquidation shall only occur at an all-time three-year high. The assumption is that the asset would have been at least doubling in value when liquidating at an all-time 3-year high. Only buy precious metal at Spot Value.

K. Buying Commodities as an asset class is allowable (suggest 5% but no more than 10%). Commodities have a low correlation to Equities and Fixed Income; however, they have volatility like Equities but a low return comparable to U.S. Short-Term Government Bonds. Commodities as an Asset Class are only valuable in reducing the portfolio's volatility through diversification.

L. When Nations and Countries fall, their paper currency becomes worthless. The financial currency markets are resilient and will adopt the world's most stable and safest currency as an alternative. Precious Metals will retain their purchasing power.

M. Beware of the fear mongers; for the Financial Markets to fail and no longer function (where all investments equal a negative return), a Global Catastrophic Risk or Human Existential Risk will have to occur. The Principal / Agent will only have an expensive IOU if such events occur. The portfolio valuation will be the least of the Principal / Agent concerns; basic survival will be paramount. If humanity survives, the economy will eventually return to a barter trade system for goods/services. As stability develops, Precious Metals will again become the currency of commerce.

N. If the Principal / Agent chooses to buy U.S. Government Debt Securities directly, the Principal / Agent shall consider buying from "U. S. Treasury Direct" with no more than seven-year maturity. Faith in the U.S. Government has diminished significantly due to an ever-increasing national debt without a gold/silver/platinum standard; I suggest investing no more than 10%.

O. Derivatives are highly discouraged unless the following objectives are achievable—reduce risk and increase return. If those goals are not in writing and there is no guarantee from the brokerage or investment firm, then authorization for using derivatives will not occur. Due to the various variables and external factors, derivatives can be incredibly complex and complicated; thus, determining a fair market value can be difficult.

P. The use of Hedge Funds as a means of asset allocation is highly discouraged unless the following objectives are achievable – reduce risk and increase return overall for the entire investment portfolio. If those goals are not in writing with a brokerage or investment firm guarantee, then Hedge Funds will not be authorized. Hedge Funds as an Asset Allocation shall only be 7 - 10% of the total investment portfolio value if the Fiduciary decides to be adventurous.

Q. When a Financial Advisor suggests a Mutual Fund or ETF to fulfill a role within a Portfolio, the Principal / Agent shall request the following free of charge. Based on the Time Horizon in question, a Net Present Value Analysis shall determine the appropriate investment(s) (and potential alternatives). This Net Present Value Analysis shall consider the following factors: Expense Ratio, Front Load, Deferred Load, Annual Percentage Load, 12b-1 Fee, Management Fee, Taxes, and Turnover Rate. The Net Present Value analysis shall be in an Excel Spreadsheet. The Excel Spreadsheet shall also have an attached Monte Carlo Analysis so the Fiduciary can determine the "sensitivity exposure" based on the return history for the security in question with a Value at Risk (VAR) based on the Monte Carlo Analysis with Confidence Intervals.

R. Every quarter, the entire investment portfolio (if managed by a Fiduciary) shall have a report indicating Aggregate Sharpe & Sortino Ratio, investment portfolio Beta/Alpha, and Value at Risk (VAR) on the Monte Carlo Analysis with Confidence Intervals.

05. Pay for the required financial advice or service, not all the extras.

06. When the financial planner recommends an investment, ask if there is a penalty for getting the money back. If so, ask for details (how much, how long). Liquidation or transferal penalties are indicators that the financial planner is getting a commission, usually a big one.

07. Ask the financial planner to justify why this is an appropriate or suitable investment for the Principal / Agent and the total expense that will occur. Ensure that gross expenses are less than one percent annually. Walk away if the financial planner refuses.

08. Does the Principal / Agent understand all aspects of the investment? How do these investments fit the strategy and goals that the Principal wants to achieve? Explain the investment to someone trustworthy to test one's understanding and ask that person for feedback.

09. Have the Financial Planner explain their compensation method – Fee-Only, Commission, and Percentage of Asset Under Management.

10. Reflect on how the financial planner and the product's issuer can get rich and how these products benefit the consumer.

Principal: ______

S. The Fiduciary shall rebalance (no less than quarterly) the corpus assets to comply with the asset allocations (Country, Sector, and Size) as previously agreed and shall review the holdings and follow the **5/25% rule** in making appropriate changes. Furthermore, tax minimization strategies should be considered when rebalancing.

T. When evaluating the Fiduciary's performance, consider the following: Did the Fiduciary outperform a weighted market index benchmark? Did the Fiduciary create any additional economic value to the investment portfolio? Furthermore, how does the Fiduciary deserve the Principal's money for a service / managerial fee? Keep this example in mind: Assume an investment portfolio of $100,000.00, and at the end of one year, the investment portfolio had a market value of $120,000.00; thus, the portfolio grew by $20,000.00 or 20%; the weighted index market benchmark was 10%. How much compensation should the Fiduciary get if the Fiduciary outperforms the weighted index?
Professionally managed investment portfolios usually impose a reasonable and prudent fee of 1% or less. Please think about the following statement: should the managerial fee percentage apply to the gross investment portfolio or just the incremental growth of the investment portfolio? One percent of the total investment portfolio will be $1,200.00, but 1% of the additional growth of the portfolio will be $200.00. From a logical and rational perspective, the Principal / Agent could have invested the money and kept up with the inflation rate. Thus, the only value that the Fiduciary has achieved was an incremental growth of $20,000.00 and $10,000.00 of said growth the Principal / Agent could have done without the need for a Financial Manager. Sure, the Fiduciary deserves more than just $200.00; however, how is the Fiduciary justified in having $1,200.00? Make sure to negotiate the fees for the services based on performance; failure is grounds for incompetence. Remember, the more money the Fiduciary skims at the top, the less money for the Principal, so be greedy; that is the Principal's money. Consider doing a break-even analysis when comparing financial transactions, including the financial reports and sought-after financial advice, and then choose the course that best benefits the Principal as the investor. Remember, the Fiduciary money is not at risk in the markets; the Fiduciary paycheck is guaranteed at the Principal's expense regardless of what happens unless the Principal / Agent dictates terms otherwise.

U. Remember, wealth on the "Books" differs from wealth "In the Wallet," so the Principal's investment is at risk until the Principal has the money in their bank account.

V. Beware of Market Bubbles. When perception exceeds reality regarding an asset's worth, a Market Bubble occurs - when in a Market Bubble, sell off the inflated asset and do not buy the asset. This financial advice is easier to give than to achieve.

W. Beware of companies that sell a lifestyle, thus promising the sun, stars, and the moon. These companies tend to be Multilevel Marketing or a deviation thereof. These companies can easily be a front for a sophisticated Pyramid or Ponzi scheme. Thus, it is advisable to be very skeptical. These companies usually share the following traits: **(01)** private companies with minimal regulations or oversight. **(02)** Lack of financial disclosure. **(03)** Focuses on recruitment versus sales. **(04)** Requires the purchase of inventory to maintain a particular status or position. **(05)** Sell products with "Miraculous Claims" that have no credible scientific proof of their validity or are not peer-reviewed.

X. Remember, ownership of wealth is an illusion. Might make right, unless might is too poor to fight. The Government can always take away one's land, material wealth, or freedom, especially if a person is a threat, disruptive force, or political obstacle. When a person pays a recurring tax on free and simple property, does that person truly own that property? Can one truly own property if a third party wants one's property and uses the legal system to take it, using civil asset forfeiture, eminent domain, nationalization, et cetera.?

Y. Oprah Winfrey said it best: "Sign your own checks." Many wealthy/ famous people have delegated their financial rights/responsibilities to another for convenience purposes and live to regret it. It is easy for a "money manager" to go wild shit-crazy with the Principal's money and spend or use the funds in unapproved ways. Be forewarned when dealing with a sleazy money manager; lawsuits tend to be very costly, litigious, and time-consuming, so it is best to avoid trouble.

11. Ask the financial planner whether any certificates of deposit (CD) or money-market accounts (preferably back by the U.S. government) are currently paying more than the bonds or cash-like assets. Verify the yields at **depositaccounts.com** or **bankrate.com** to see if the financial planner is correct.

12. Watch for these warning signs: Is the financial product or service too good to be true? Does the investment promise high returns or state that the investment is "risk-free?" Does the Financial Planner request that the Principal / Agent sign a document saying that the Principal / Agent has reviewed many pages and understood the contents? Does the Financial Planner boast or make predictions about beating the financial market? Is the financial planner trying to build or establish trust from religious affiliations? Does the financial planner use sales pressure techniques such as the Principal / Agent must sign in the next 24 or 48 hours?

13. Do not trust solely based on references. Trust Numbers. Trust assets under management in comparison to similar financial institutions. Trust one's gut feeling. Remember, the worst financial planners can still find people who will recommend using their services.

Principal: ______

Z. The Fiduciary shall also adhere to the following corollaries of the Prudent Investor Rule:

- A Fiduciary must verify information concerning the investment/ management of the estate or trust assets.
- An Investor shall hire and rely upon a Fiduciary only after due diligence, care, and review of the credentials and performance of the individual or firm.
- The Fiduciary must diversify investments unless there are extraordinary circumstances or directions to the contrary.
- The Fiduciary must consider many factors in investing and managing the property. Some are predictable: **(01)** General Economic Conditions; **(02)** The possible effect of inflation, stagnation, or deflation; **(03)** The expected or foreseen tax consequences of an investment decision; **(04)** The anticipated total return (income plus price appreciation) of each asset.
- A Fiduciary is to consider various external resources for the investor/beneficiaries. **(01)** Consideration factors regarding a particular asset that may have unique value or sentimental meaning for a beneficiary. (**02**) Are there any advantages to changing the asset's ownership to a trust? (**03**) Is the asset for the benefit of multiple beneficiaries? **(04)** Is there a need for regular income streams versus the potential for investment growth?

AA. It is vitally important that the Principal / Agent change their mindset regarding creating and managing wealth. Suggested reading: **(01)** **Money: Master the Game** by **Tony Robbins**. **(02)** **Rich Dad, Poor Dad** by **Robert T. Kiyosaki**. **(03)** **The Richest Man in Babylon** by **George S. Clason**. **(04)** **The Millionaire Next Door** by **Thomas Stanley** & **William Danko**.

BB. For additional information regarding investing, suggest reading the following books written or co-written by **Larry E. Swedroe**: **(01)** **The Only Guide to Winning Investment Strategy You'll Ever Need: Index Funds and Beyond**. **(02)** **The Only Guide to a Winning Bond Strategy You'll Ever Need**. **(03)** **The Only Guide to Alternative Investments You'll Ever Need**.

CC. Upon amassing a fortune, be proactive to ensure the Principal benefits from their wealth from various potential threats. Suggested reading the following: **(01)** **A Guide to Asset Protection: How to Keep What's Legally Yours** by **Robert F. Krueger**. **(02)** **The Tax & Legal Playbook** by **Mark J. Kohler**.

DD. As mentioned earlier, the principal / Agent can purchase the book(s) cheaply and in used condition using this website: **www.dealoz.com**. This website searches over **20,000** online stores to find the best deal possible.

EE. Historically and currently, there is a symbolic tether of material wealth to social status and elevation; this is incredibly short-sighted, shallow, and myopic thinking. However, society still holds onto these conventions due to the instinctual desire for material wealth, greed, and increased mating opportunities. Remember that having lots of wealth will not give a person love, peace, joy, success, or meaning to one's life. A person's impact on society, family, and friends is the actual value of a person's life - money is a tool, so use it wisely to ensure an enduring legacy.

14. Learn the strengths & weaknesses of the Financial Planner. Some Financial Planners specialize in Retirement Planning, Business Operations, Tax Reduction & Avoidance, High Net Worth Individuals, Young Professionals, et cetera.

15. Choose a Financial Planner with a compatible strategy that complements one's investment style and risk tolerance.

16. Be patient; do not hire the first Financial Planner you meet. Shop around, learn, inquire, and interview before hiring a Financial Planner.

17. If it sounds too good to be true, it is - odds are 98% of it is false.

18. There is no "Risk-Free" or "Guarantee." Do not be duped, and do not suffer a liar.

Principal: ________

This page is intentionally left blank

Attorney Suggestions & Resource Guide

Attorney Suggestions & Resource Guide

Step 01: Attorney Selection

- Ask a friend, family, and associates for recommendations regarding Attorneys in the local area.
- Utilize an Attorney referral service; their contact information is usually in a phone directory under "Attorney Referral Service" or "Attorneys." This service is generally provided by the Bar Association (check their website), with the sole purpose of matching clients with a licensed Attorney (hopefully in good standing) to their particular legal needs. A referral service will not guarantee the quality of work, experience, or the Attorney's abilities.
- If the Attorney is worth their salt, their contact information will be in the local phone directory. Look at the display advertisement to indicate an Attorney's area of practice or expertise.
- Ask another Attorney for a recommended referral (provided the Attorney does not specialize in that particular area of the law), especially if that Attorney has had past dealings.

Step 02: Attorney Evaluation

- Select between three (**03**) to five (**05**) Attorneys worthy of further consideration. Call each Attorney's office and ask the following questions: (**01**) Does the Attorney practice or handle cases regarding the legal issue? (**02**) How much will the legal expenses cost? How soon can an Attorney appointment be available?
- If the answers to the previous question were favorable, request to speak to the Attorney (via phone or by appointment) and ask the Attorney the following questions: How much will the legal expense be (a written estimate is preferred), and what payment methods are available? How long has the Attorney been practicing law? Does the Attorney have experience with this type of legal issue? How long will it take before the Client sees any results?
- If the answers to the previous question were favorable, then internally ask: (**01**) As a potential client, is the Attorney personable? (**02**) Is the Attorney friendly and understanding? (**03**) Does the Attorney exhibit confident behavior? (**04**) Is the Attorney straightforward and able to communicate and explain things? If the answers to the previous question were favorable, the Attorney is a good fit overall.

Step 03: Working with an Attorney

- Ask questions, especially if the Client wants to know something or does not understand something. Do not feel embarrassed by asking questions relevant to the legal case. Remember, an Attorney is not a mind reader. If the Attorney is not willing to take the time to explain the processes involved or answer legal questions within a week, then it may be time to look for a new Attorney.
- Provide complete information on the case or legal issue. Conversations with the Attorney are confidential. If an Attorney discloses information without the Client's consent, the Attorney can lose their license to practice law. The Attorney will tell the Client what is realistic and offer pragmatic options to achieve one legal goal(s). Listen attentively to what the Attorney says and accept how the law and the legal system operate. The Attorney has no control over the following: (**01**) how the legal system works or (**02**) the wording of laws. However, an Attorney can be creative in finding solutions to a client's legal problem; thus, it is advantageous to keep an open mind to alternative suggestions.
- Be patient; do not be in such a hurry. Unless the Client is paying an Attorney a considerable chunk of money, do not expect the Attorney to be at one's immediate disposal. Most Attorneys are extremely busy and overworked while maintaining a large caseload; thus, be patient and understanding.
- Utilize the Attorney's Secretary. The Attorney's Secretary (paralegal) is an invaluable resource a client can utilize. It behooves the Client to be friendly and get to know the Secretary. The Secretary will often answer the Client's questions both freely and quickly.
- Keep the legal case moving - make the case squeak. As the saying goes, "The loudest squeak gets the most oil." this is also true for an Attorney's services. Procrastination of legal work is commonplace until the deadline is near, an emergency develops, or a client calls; this tends to be an occupational hazard in the law profession. Attorneys, in general, take on more cases than recommended with the desire to earn a more significant income. The Client's goal is to make a loud squeak, but not too much that the Attorney would rather avoid the Client. When talking to the Attorney, ask the following questions: (**01**) What is the next step in the process? (**02**) What is the projected timeframe for completion? (**03**) When should one schedule a follow-up call or appointment? (**04**) If the Client does not hear from their Attorney at a designated time, call the next day and be cordial and understanding.

Attorney Suggestions & Resource Guide

Step 04: How to Save Money when Using an Attorney

- Think relative and proportional. Do not hire an Attorney for $500 an hour when a $100 an hour Attorney will do; thus, buy the skill, not the name. Sometimes, a shrewd negotiator or a logical, methodical Attorney is better.
- Negotiate for a Flat Fee or an alternative billing model, and make sure it is in writing.
- Carefully craft and consider the questions for the Attorney and keep phone calls to a minimum; when paying hourly, it is best to keep the conversation short, brief, and concise. An email response is usually a better option.
- Use the Secretary whenever possible; the Secretary may know some of the law, status, and case information and can give a more proactive status update for free. If the Secretary cannot answer the question, the Attorney will respond as time allows.
- Review the invoice/bill carefully, scrutinize it, and ask for clarification whenever necessary. The bill should be clear and concise, explaining the litigation work; watch out for hidden expenses.
- The more knowledgeable the Client is concerning the legal topic, the more useful the Client is to the Attorney and thus the more intelligent the question will be. If an unscrupulous Attorney considers the Client naïve or ignorant, the odds of being hoodwinked increase; thus, knowledge is the great equalizer. Consider visiting the following website: **www.Lawers.com, www.Avvo.com, www.Expertlaw.com, www.scholar.google.com, www.Nolo.com, www.Justia.com,** and **www.FindLaw.com.**
- Be prepared for appointments. As the Client, make it a priority to have all paperwork in order and available. Plan when consulting with the Attorney; get straight to the point; chitchat is unnecessary. Outline the discussion topics and ask questions in advance.
- If legal document preparation services are required, consider service providers such as **www.LegalZoom.com**, **www.RocketLawyer.com**, and **www.LawDepot.com**; these websites will help prepare basic legal documents for a minimal cost and allow general legal questions to be answered free of charge. However, Legal documents are usually oversimplified and not tailored to the unique needs and situations in life or business.
- Consider using the Small Claims Court, which is usually cheaper, and legal representation is optional.
- Be proactive and do some of the legwork. As the Client asks the Attorney what the Client can do to minimize the legal expense, some examples include picking up and delivering paperwork.
- Consider using Mediation or Arbitration. Mediation is preferable when the parties (neighbors, family members, or clients/small businesses) have a stake in staying on good future terms. Arbitration is more decisive and less expensive than a lawsuit. However, arbitration is usually binding, thus not appealable, and requires hiring an Attorney and paying legal fees.
- Try bargaining or service swapping. Small legal firms and solo practitioners are more likely to consider this type of arrangement, especially if the Client offers a service that the Attorney finds of value. Like any business, there are expenses, and if the Client can decrease those expenses or increase revenue, then the Attorney is more applicable to such a service trade arrangement. Consider visiting these websites: **www.barterquest.com, www.swapright.com, www.u-exchange.com,** and even **www.craigslist.com**. Remember, for a service trade arrangement to work, it should be the following: preferably in written format, with details that are clear and concise, and with equal consideration exchanging for the services. **Please Note:** If legal expenses exceed the service's value, seek tax advice from an accountant (CPA) or tax professional when bartering in advance.

Step 05: Paying the Attorney

- Money Talks - If the Client pays their legal fees on time or before it is due, rest assured that the Attorney will give prompt attention and services.
- Ask for an itemized bill showing what the Attorney did and how long it took.
- The Attorney may ask for a retainer in advance; if this occurs, ensure the terms are in writing with a timeline for the goals/objectives.

Step 06: Discharging the Attorney

- If the Client can no longer trust or work with the Attorney, it is time to end the Client/Attorney relationship.
- Make sure to send a letter to the Attorney stating that their services are not required, thus discharging the Attorney from the case or services.
- Remember to stop by the Attorney's office to pick up the files (copies of papers already prepared and billed for and any documents the Client has provided). If the Attorney refuses to give the Client their file, contact the Bar Association and file a complaint or grievance.
- Settle any remaining Attorney's fees owed.

This page is intentionally left blank

Steps for Credit Repair & Debt Statute of Limitations

Steps for Credit Repair

Steps for Repairing Credit:

- **Review your Credit History:**
  - Get a copy of your free **Credit Report** at **http://www.annualcreditreport.com** and download each credit report from the following credit agencies: Transunion, Equifax, and Experian.
  - Lexis Nexis is a massive data repository and aggregator of personal information; thus, request your **Consumer Report** at **https://consumer.risk.lexisnexis.com/request**.
  - Review credit reports (Transunion, Equifax, and Experian) and consumer reports (Lexis Nexis) for errors and adverse/negative claims and dispute all claims. The creditor must prove that the debt is legitimate.
  - All adverse/negative claims on a credit report drop off after ten (**10**) years. If the debt is older than ten (**10**) years and still shows on your credit report - dispute it, and it will drop off. The Statute of Limitations starts on the default date, usually when the creditor receives the last payment.
  - Never acknowledge a debt or pay a debt with a debt collector. Look up the state's Statute of Limitations law regarding credit card debt. If the debt is older than the Statute of Limitations with no Judgment/Lien at the Recorder's / County Clerk's office, that debt is unenforceable; this is a Time-Barred Debt.
  - If you acknowledge a debt or even make a payment on a debt past the Statute of Limitations, the debt collector can revive the debt (Zombie Debt) and make it legitimate and enforceable again. That is why you do not claim the debt or even make a payment. Why do you think debt collectors record all conversations?
  - Never give out financial or employment information to a debt collector. If you do so, expect wage garnishment and bank/financial levies.
- **Look up Judgment/Lien:**
  - A Judgment/Lien is the legal method used to intercept and satisfy any default debt, usually from the sale of real estate or probated inheritance.
  - Go to the Recorder's / County Clerk's office and research if you have any Judgment/Lien filed against you. Look up the state's Statute of Limitations law regarding Judgment/Lien, the duration period, and the ability to renew. If you plan to buy property in one state, only concern yourself with counties in that state you lived in within the last fifteen (**15**) years. Every state varies regarding the Statute of Limitations for Credit Card Debt and Judgment/Lien.
  - If you have a Judgment/Lien against you, verify the debt. If it is not your debt, contact a lawyer (usually, a bankruptcy lawyer will do it).
- **Paying on Debt or Judgment/Lien:**
  - If the debt is legitimate, you can do the following: one (**01**) wait and hope the debt expires and does not renew, or two (**02**) you can negotiate/settle the debt. Suggest that you offer 15% to 25% of the balance as a lump sum owed on the debt - make sure that everything is in writing (verbal promises are worthless).
  - In writing, ensure that the Debt collector agrees to relinquish all assignment rights if you negotiate/settle a debt. Failure to do so may result in the creditor selling the unrecovered debt to another debt collector.
  - Recommend paying a debt in full if the debt has no Judgment/Lien and is still younger than five (**05**) years. However, you can always gamble and wait to see if the creditor chooses to pursue a Judgment/Lien.
  - If the debt or Judgment/Lien is on your Credit Report, before paying the debt off – make sure in writing that the deletion of the said adverse claim will occur upon successfully satisfying the Debt or Judgment/Lien. If you are paying on a Judgment/Lien, request a release of Judgment/Lien mailed to your address within one month. You must file the release with the Recorder's / County Clerk's office.
  - Always use a check when paying a debt collector, give the money to another person you trust (with no default debt), and have them write the check on your behalf. Make sure in the memo section you write the account number of the debt in question, and on the back, preferably above the signature line, write the following: "Settle/Paid in Full." If you write a check to a debt collector with your bank/financial account information, you give the debt collector all the required information to wipe out your bank/financial account. Remember, if the Debt collector does not cash the check, the debt collector does not have to honor any written or verbal agreement.
  - Joint Bank/Financial accounts are subject to levy, so if you owe a significant debt, it will be prudent not to have a high balance.

Principal: ________

- **Default Student Loan Debt:**
  - This debt is impossible to eliminate except for the following: (**01**) victim of fraud by a College or University or (**02**) permanently physically or mentally disabled, thus receiving a disability check from the government.
  - Private Default Student Loan Debt issued through a Bank/Financial Institution (not the State/Federal Government) can receive a discharge through bankruptcy.
  - Default Student Loan Debt does not have a Statute of Limitations; however, garnishment is usually a cap as a percentage of discretionary income. Furthermore, this debt can be at the Federal or State level, with each having different rules regarding computation and withholding of the garnishment amounts. Moreover, both debts are subject to Tax Refund intercept. Tax Intercept and Wage Garnishment priority goes as follows: Child Support → Alimony → Tax Debt → Default Student Loan Debt → Non-Taxable Debt (Government Debt → Credit Card Debt → Medical Debt).
  - Typically, filing and recording a Judgment/Lien for default Student Loan Debt does not occur at the Recorder's / County Clerk's office. Because the debt-collecting agency can easily intercept tax refunds, implement pay garnishment, and impose a bank/financial levy default without needing a Judgment/Lien.
- **Bankruptcy:**
  - Bankruptcy should only be an option if you are in significant debt and will not pay it off within ten (**10**) years. Think of it as $100,000.00 or more. Furthermore, discharging Default Student Loan debt that is State or Federal back is almost impossible in bankruptcy. Consult a licensed bankruptcy attorney to evaluate if bankruptcy is right for you.
  - Chapter 7 bankruptcy will reflect on your credit report for ten (**10**) years, and Chapter 13 will reflect for seven (**07**) years. If you file for bankruptcy, you receive a clean slate because creditors know you cannot file again for an extended period.
- **Applying for Loan/Mortgage:**
  - Just because a debt is no longer on your credit report does not mean you still do not have legal obligations to pay for it. When applying for a loan/mortgage, the financial institution will examine your cash flow to determine if you have enough discretionary income to pay said loan/mortgage. The applicant must provide employment verification and up to six (**06**) months' worth of payroll information to receive a loan/mortgage.
  - The financial institution will exclude the following debts when calculating a mortgage's debt-to-income (**DTI**):
    - Debts paid off within ten (**10**) months of the mortgage closing date.
    - Debts such as utility and medical bills that are not shown in a credit report.
    - Debts paid by other individuals must be able to prove that payments were made on time for at least twelve (**12**) months. Bank Statements or canceled checks are acceptable forms of proof.
- **Credit Card Use:**
  - To have a credit history, you must have debt use. If you currently use a debit card, consider applying for a credit card with the same financial institution. The easiest way to establish a credit history is to get a credit card with a $1,000.00 limit using no more than 30%. Use the credit card to make everyday purchases; if possible, pay it off before the statement (closing) date to prevent paying interest. Do not take cash advances.
  - Numerous factors determine a credit score. To achieve a high credit score, do the following: have a low utilization ratio, pay it off monthly, and maintain all credit lines even if you do not use them unless they charge an inactivity fee. There are many tips, but these are the major ones.
  - To prevent identity theft and to prevent unauthorized use of credit cards or loans, I suggest implementing a credit freeze (which is free) at Transunion, Equifax, and Experian. Thus, if you want another line of credit, you must provide a security code to unfreeze the account when applying for said credit line or loan.

Debt Statute of Limitations

Debt Statute of Limitations:

A statute of limitation gives a creditor the right to take legal action against you in a specific timeframe, thus asking the court to force you to pay a debt. The court system does not keep track of the status of your debt. Instead, you must prove the debt has passed its statute of limitation. Furthermore, most States give the Creditors the right to renew a Judgment/Lien, thus extending the Statute of Limitations. This is accomplished by filing a renewal notice with a Recorder's / County Clerk's office, implementing a wage garnishment order with an employer, or implementing a financial levy order with a financial institution.

Principal: ________

Time-Barred Debt:

Time-Barred debt is debt that has passed the statute of limitation. However, just because the debts have aged past the statute of limitation does not mean that you no longer owe money or that your credit rating has not suffered. This means the creditor will not get a judgment/Lien against you if you come to court prepared with proof that your debt is too old. Proof might include a personal check showing the last time you made a payment or records of communication that you have made about that debt.

Categories of Debt:

Debt falls into one of four categories. Knowing your debt type is essential because their time limits vary. If you have doubts, check with your attorney about your debt type.

- **Oral Agreements:** These are debts created via a verbal agreement to pay back the money, and nothing is in writing.
- **Written Contracts:** These debts come with a signed contract (on paper – napkin counts) by you and a third party. A written contract usually includes the terms and conditions of the loan, such as the loan amount and the monthly payment. Medical debt is also considered a written contract.
- **Promissory Notes:** A promissory note is a written agreement to pay back debt at a specific interest rate and by a certain date and time. Mortgages and student loans are two examples of promissory notes.
- **Open-Ended Accounts:** An open-ended account has a revolving balance you can repay and then borrow again. Credit cards, in-store credit, and lines of credit are all examples of open-ended accounts. However, an account is not open-ended if you can only borrow the money one (**01**) time.

Each state has its statute of limitations on debt, which varies depending on your debt type. Usually, it is between three (**03**) and six (**06**) years, but it can be as high as ten (**10**) or fifteen (**15**) years. Before responding to a debt collection, determine your state's statute of limitations. If the statute of limitations has passed, you may have less incentive to pay the debt. If the credit-reporting time limit (a date independent of the statute of limitations) has passed, you may be even less inclined to pay the debt. These are the statutes of limitation, measured by years, in each state as of **June 2019**. **Please Note:** State laws and statutes are subject to change.

State	Oral	Written	Promissory	Open	State	Oral	Written	Promissory	Open
Alabama	6	6	6	3	Montana	5	8	8	5
Alaska	3	3	3	3	Nebraska	4	5	5	4
Arizona	3	6	6	3	Nevada	4	6	3	4
Arkansas	3	5	3	3	New Hampshire	3	3	6	3
California	2	4	4	4	New Jersey	6	6	6	6
Colorado	6	6	6	6	New Mexico	4	6	6	4
Connecticut	3	6	6	3	New York	6	6	6	6
Delaware	3	3	3	4	North Carolina	3	3	5	3
Florida	4	5	5	4	North Dakota	6	6	6	6
Georgia	4	6	6	6	Ohio	6	8	15	6
Hawaii	6	6	6	6	Oklahoma	3	5	5	3
Idaho	4	5	5	5	Oregon	6	6	6	6
Illinois	5	10	10	5	Pennsylvania	4	4	4	4
Indiana	6	6	10	6	Rhode Island	10	10	10	10
Iowa	5	10	5	5	South Carolina	3	3	3	3
Kansas	3	5	5	3	South Dakota	6	6	6	6
Kentucky	5	10	15	5	Tennessee	6	6	6	6
Louisiana	10	10	10	3	Texas	4	4	4	4
Maine	6	6	6	6	Utah	4	6	6	4
Maryland	3	3	6	3	Vermont	6	6	5	3
Massachusetts	6	6	6	6	Virginia	3	5	6	3
Michigan	6	6	6	6	Washington	3	6	6	3
Minnesota	6	6	6	6	West Virginia	5	10	6	5
Mississippi	3	3	3	3	Wisconsin	6	6	10	6
Missouri	5	10	10	5	Wyoming	8	10	10	8

Principal: ________

Glossary

Glossary

Accounts Receivable are the money an individual or entity owes on selling the product(s) or service(s) on credit.

Administrator is a court-appointed person with fiduciary powers to administer the estate of a deceased person with no Will.

Advance Directive is a legal document in which a person specifies what health-related actions would occur if that person were to become incapacitated or incompetent.

Affidavit is a written declaration or statement that a person swears or affirms under the penalty of perjury.

Agent is a person who serves as a Fiduciary on behalf of the Principal. The Agent creates legal relations with third parties by a Power of Attorney. The Agent may be a Subservient Agent to a Protector.

Annuity is an insurance product that provides a series of payments to a person at fixed intervals, for the duration of a person's remaining life span.

Arbitration is an alternative dispute resolution method that resolves disputes outside the judiciary courts.

Arbitrator is an independent person who receives an appointment to serve in a capacity to settle a dispute in Arbitration.

Assign is the legal term for transferring rights, property, or other benefits procured under a contract to another party.

Attorney-In-Fact: read the definition of Agent.

Beneficiary is a person or other legal entity who receives money, property, or other benefits from another party. Source: barnesgroupbenefits.com

Bill of Exchange is a negotiable instrument that requires one party to pay a fixed sum of money to another party on demand or in the future. Source: byjus.com and Investopedia.com

Bond (Legal) is a written agreement between two parties in which one party receives money and the other promises to engage in specific acts; failure to perform those acts results in the forfeiture of previously given money.

Bond (Financial) is a type of financial security in which the debtor promises to pay the creditor. The repayment structure of the debt occurs in a manner that disburses interest in a defined amount at a defined set interval over a specified timeframe, with the return of the initial monetary amount at the end.

Brokerage is a person or firm that arranges a financial transaction between a buyer and a seller for a commission by executing an order.

Buy on Margin: read the definition of Margin.

Call is a contract to exchange security at a set price between the buyer and seller of a call option. The buyer has the right but not the obligation to buy the commodity or financial security; conversely, the seller is obligated to sell the commodity if the buyer decides to enforce the contract. Source: sec.gov

Call Options: read the definition of Call.

Capital Gain is the profits earned on the sale of an asset, which has increased in value over time.

Certificate of Deposit (CD) is a time deposit of money commonly sold by banks, savings and loan associations, and credit unions. In this type of deposit, a person sells cash for some time in exchange for interest.

Codicil is a legal document that changes an existing WILL through amendments, which may alter, explain, add to, subtract from, or confirm provisions within a WILL.

Collateral is the property that a borrower pledges to a lender to secure the repayment of a loan.

Commodity is a physical good, usually a resource with characteristics that are the same. The financial markets treat these physical goods as equivalent regardless of the good's producer.

Complex POA is an Author's term for a Power of Attorney designed for long-term (greater than five years) use with multiple Agents and optional safety features.

Conservator is a court-appointed person supervising an Incapacitated or Incompetent Adult's financial affairs, health care, or living arrangements.

Conservatorship involves appointing a Conservator to serve in a fiduciary capacity, managing a person's financial affairs, health care, or living arrangements.

Co-tenancy is the designation status of ownership in property that more than one person owns at a time. Examples of Co-tenancy include Tenancy in Common, Joint Tenancy, Joint Tenancy with Rights of Survivorship, and Tenancy by the Entirety.

Custodian is a person designated to hold and manage property for the benefit of another person, usually a minor child.

Custodian of Record is an individual or entity (Court or County Clerk) that has custody (possession) of important records, also known as a "Record Custodian."

Declarant is a person or party who makes a formal declaration.

Declaration is a written statement usually presented as evidence to a Judge in Court in which the writer (Declarant) swears under penalty of perjury that the contents are accurate and true. A Judge will utilize a declaration to determine the Declarant's intent, especially when the Declarant is either incompetent or incapacitated.

Deed of Trust is a type of mortgage. The borrower signs a promissory note indicating that the real property is collateral to secure the debt owed to the lender. The borrower then signs a deed of Trust, which transfers the land to the lender until repayment. Source: realtytrac.com and digitalcommons.law.uw.edu

Defendant may be an individual, company, or institution accused of a crime or sued in a court.

Deferred Compensation Plan is an account usually reserved for retirement in which a person withholds a portion of their pay until a specified date in the future; examples include but are not limited to, the following: pensions, 401(k) retirement plans, and employee stock options. A deferred compensation plan may be either a Qualified or Non-Qualified plan. Read the definition of a Non-Qualified Retirement Plan and Qualified Retirement Plan.

Defined Benefit Plan is an employer-based program that pays a fixed, pre-established benefit for employees at retirement, usually based on factors such as length of employment and salary history.

Defined Contribution Plan is an employer-based program in which an employee contributes money, and the employer typically makes a matching contribution up to a certain percentage. Three popular types of these plans are 401(k), 403(b), and 457.

Delegate is an Author's term for a person (non-acting Agent) that serves on behalf of the acting Agent currently in power, thus a Subservient Agent.

Deposit Instruments is an investment in an interest-bearing account or short-term interest-bearing security.

Dissolution of Marriage is the formal legal term for the legal ending of a marriage by a court, commonly called a divorce.

Dividends are a distribution of profits or surplus by a corporation to its shareholders.

Durable Clause is additional legal language incorporated into a Power of Attorney that maintains enforceability if the Principals become incompetent or incapacitated.

Durable POA is the Author's term for a Power of Attorney designed for long-term (greater than five years) use with multiple Agents and optional safety features. The primary key difference that separates a Durable POA from a Complex POA is that the durability provisions are already active.

Durability Clause: read the definition of the Durable Clause.

Duress is a legal term that refers to threats, violence, constraints, or other action brought to bear on someone to do something against their will or better judgment.

Easement is a legal term that refers to the right to cross or otherwise use someone else's land for a specified purpose.

Employee Benefit Plan is an employer-based program that provides medical, health, and hospitalization benefits or income if the employee suffers from sickness, accident, or death.

Employee Retirement Income Security Act (ERISA) is a federal United States tax and labor law establishing minimum standards for private industry pension plans. It contains rules on the federal income tax effects of transactions associated with employee benefit plans. Source: govtrack.us and Investopedia.com

Employee Savings Plan is an employer-based program with a pooled investment account in which the employer usually matches the contributions, comparable to a Defined Contribution Plan.

Employee Welfare Plan: Read the definition of Employee Benefit Plan.

Encumbrance is a third party's right to, interest in, or legal liability on property that may hinder the property owner's ability to transfer title or diminish the property's value.

Equity: read the definition of Stock.

Estate is a person's net worth at any time, alive or dead; it is the sum of a person's assets – legal rights, interest, and entitlements to property of any kind – less all liabilities at that time. Source: kdanc.com and Wikipedia.org

Glossary

Estate Planning is the process of designating who will receive a person's assets in the event of death or incapacitation. With the help of legal and tax professionals, the goal is to ensure heirs and beneficiaries receive assets in a way that manages and minimizes taxes such as estate and gift taxes. Source: nerdwallet.com

Estate Tax is a federal tax levied on the net value of the estate of a deceased person before distribution to the heirs.

Exchange-Traded Fund (ETF) is a "basket" of securities that tracks an underlying index; unlike a mutual fund, the computation of ETF's NAV occurs throughout the trading day and can be bought and sold like a Stock. Actively managed ETFs do exist. Source: Investopedia.com

Executor is a person that the Testator nominates to carry out the instructions of a WILL. The executor's duties also include disbursing property to the beneficiaries as designated in the will, obtaining information about potential heirs, collecting and arranging for payment of debts of the estate, and approving or disapproving creditors' claims.

Family Educational Rights and Privacy Act (FERPA) is a United States federal law governing access to educational information and records by public entities such as potential employers, publicly funded educational institutions, and foreign governments. Source: Wikipedia.org

Fiduciary is a person or organization that acts on behalf of another individual and is legally bound to act solely in their best interest. Source: Investopedia.com

Final Disposition is the planning, execution, and management of the bodily remains after death; this may include but is not limited to, any of the following: **(01)** arrangements for viewing, **(02)** a funeral ceremony, memorial service, graveside service, or another last rite, and **(03)** a burial, cremation, or donation.

Financial Securities: read the definition of Securities.

Fraud occurs when an individual or entity intentionally deceives another individual or entity to induce an unlawful gain or deny a right. The following are examples of diverse types of fraud: tax fraud, credit card fraud, wire fraud, securities fraud, and bankruptcy fraud.

Functioning Non-Socially is the Author's term for a person who demonstrates one or more of the following conditions: a person cannot recognize people, communicate with people, or interact with people meaningfully.

Futures are legal agreements to buy or sell a particular commodity asset or security at a predetermined price at a specified time. Futures contracts are standardized for quality and quantity to facilitate trading on a futures exchange. Source: Investopedia.com

Futures Contract: read the definition of Futures.

Gain: read the definition of Capital Gain.

Gift Tax is a tax on the transfer of property by one individual to another while receiving nothing, or less than fair market value, in return. Source: Irs.gov

Gross Negligence: read the definition of Recklessly.

Guardian is a court-appointed person supervising a minor child's financial affairs, health care, or living arrangements.

Guardianship appoints a Guardian to serve in a fiduciary capacity that involves managing a minor child's financial affairs, health care, or living arrangements.

Healthy is the Author's term for a person who exhibits capacity with complete mental competence and is thus fully capable of independent thought, actions, and social functions.

Homestead Exemption is a legal provision that helps shield a home from some creditors following the death of a homeowner's spouse or the declaration of bankruptcy. The homestead tax exemption can also provide surviving spouses with ongoing property tax relief, usually based on a graduated scale, so homes with lower assessed values benefit the most. Source: oakandashrealty.com

Homestead Rights: read the definition of Homestead Exemption.

Incapacitated is a person demonstrating one or more of the following conditions: **(01)** the person is incapable of making, participating, or communicating a decision regarding their health care. **(02)** The person cannot manage the following: their care, property, or financial affairs.

Inchoate is a state of activity or entitlement in character to be partially complete of an intended outcome or status.

Income Tax is a tax imposed on individuals or entities (taxpayers) based on their income or profits (taxable income). Source: Wikipedia.org

Incompetent is a person who demonstrates one or more of the following conditions: (**01**) The person cannot understand and appreciate the extent, nature, and probable consequences of a proposed medical and mental health decision that may or may not have life-sustaining implications. (**02**) The person cannot make an informed, intelligent decision in a reasonable amount of time. (**03**) The person cannot communicate a coherent decision no matter how simple the communication process is. (**04**) The person cannot rationally evaluate the risks and benefits of a proposed medical and mental health decision compared to the risks and benefits of alternatives to that decision.

Indemnification is the act of compensating a person for harm or loss.

Indemnification: read the definition of Indemnify.

Index is a statistical measure of change in a representative group of individual data points. Influential global financial indices include, but are not limited to, the following: the Global Dow, the NASDAQ Composite, The Dow Jones Industrial Average, and the S&P 500. Source: Wikipedia.org and finance.yahoo.com

Index Fund is a type of mutual fund or exchange-traded fund that seeks to track the return of a market index. Source: Investo.gov

Individual Retirement Account (IRA) is a tax-advantaged account for retirement savings.

Inheritance Tax is a state tax that a beneficiary pays when receiving money or property from the estate of a deceased person. Currently, only six states impose an inheritance tax: Iowa, Kentucky, Maryland, Nebraska, New Jersey, and Pennsylvania.

Insurance is a contractual agreement by which a person pays money (consideration) to a company, and the company promises to pay cash (benefit) if the person suffers an injury or dies; the company pays for the value of the lost or damaged property or a death benefit. Source: Merriam-webster.com

Intangible property is a nonphysical property. Intangible Property examples include but are not limited to, the following: (**01**) Intangible Person Property (Liquid Assets): Bank, Checking, Saving, and Cash Accounts, Certificates of Deposit, Money-Market Funds, U.S. Bill, Notes, ETF, Mutual Funds, Stocks, Bonds, Promissory Notes, and Debt Receivables. (**02**) Intellectual Property / Business: Business Interest and Ownership Rights; Copyrights, Patents, Trademarks; Royalties, License, Permits, Contractual Agreements; and Future Inheritances.

Intentionally is a state of mind that indicates that the person has deliberately acted with an intended result or engaged in conduct with the conscious objective of achieving the desired result. Intentionally is comparable to Willfully or Purposely when it comes to legal definitions. Source: Ky. Rev. Stat. § 501.020

Inter Vivos Trust: read the definition of Living Trust.

Interest is the price a person pays to borrow money or the cost a person charges, usually quoted as an annual percentage of the loan amount.

Intestate Succession is the process by which the Court will distribute a person's property according to state law if the person dies without a WILL. Rules for distribution priority usually coincide with the relative's degree of separation. In order of priority, the relatives are as follows: Spouse ➔ Children ➔ Parents ➔ Siblings ➔ Grandchildren ➔ Aunt or Uncle. Source: finance.zacks.com

Irrevocable Trust is a type of Trust where modification, amendment, or termination of its term cannot occur without the beneficiary's permission. By transferring all ownership of assets into the Trust, the Grantor effectively and legally removes their assets ownership rights. Source: Investopedia.com

Joint Tenancy is a designation status of ownership in property owned by two or more parties, the share of each passing to the other surviving party(s) without going through probate or court system. Source: Investopedia.com and lexico.com

Joint Tenancy with Right of Survivorship: read the definition of Joint Tenancy.

Joint Venture is a combination of two or more parties that seek to develop a single enterprise or project for profit, sharing the risks associated with its development.

Judge is a public official who is appointed (usually through an election process) to decide cases in a court of law.

Knowingly is a state of mind that indicates that the person is aware that their conduct is of that nature or circumstance and the probable consequences of their actions.

Glossary

Land Trust is a legal entity that takes ownership of or authority over a piece of property at the behest of the property owner. Creating a land trust is primarily for liability and privacy protections for landowners. Source: Investopedia.com

Last Will and Testament: read the definition of WILL.

Liable is when a Judge in a court of law rules that a person is legally responsible for causing damage or injury to another person; usually, that person must pay compensation (money) to the damaged or injured person.

Lien is a form of security interest granted over an item of property to secure the payment of a debt or performance of some other obligation. Read the definition of Encumbrance. Source: Wikipedia.org

Living Trust is a type of Trust that is originated and funded by an individual during their lifetime example include, but are not limited to, the following: Irrevocable life insurance trust (ILIT), Grantor-retained annuity trust (GRAT), spousal lifetime access trust (SLAT), qualified personal residence trust (QPRT), Charitable remainder trust, and a charitable lead trust. Source: Investopedia.com

Margin is the collateral that a security holder must deposit (usually with a broker or an exchange) to cover a percentage of the credit risk the holder poses for the counterparty. Source: Wikipedia.org

Medicaid is a federal and state program that helps with healthcare costs for some people with limited income and resources (low income). Medicaid offers benefits not typically covered by Medicare, including nursing home and personal care services. Source: dept.washigton.edu and stlawrencehealthsystem.org

Medical Health Surrogate: read the definition of Surrogate.

Medicare is a federal program primarily offering health insurance to Americans aged sixty-five (65) and older (Elderly). Source: definitivelifeinsurance.com

Mental Health Surrogate: read the definition of Surrogate.

Mutual Fund is a professionally managed investment fund that pools money from many investors to purchase securities; funds are either active or passive. An index fund is an example of a passively managed fund. Source: Wikipedia.org

Naked Call Options is an options strategy in which an investor writes (sells) call options on the open market without owning the underlying security. Source: Investopedia.com

Naked Put Options is an options strategy in which the investor writes or sells Put Options without holding a short position in the underlying security. Source: Investopedia.com

Negligently is a state of mind that indicates that the person failed to exercise or act, in the given circumstances, a degree of care that a person of ordinary prudence would exercise under similar circumstances. Source: gillandchamas.com

Negotiable Paper is a transferable, signed document that promises to pay a specified person (bearer) or the assignee a sum of money (payment) at a future date or on demand.

Net Asset Value (NAV) is a computed value comprising a company's assets minus its liabilities. It is commonly associated with Mutual Funds and Exchange-Traded Funds.

Nonqualified Retirement Plan is an employer-based tax-deferred program that falls outside the Employee Retirement Income Security Act (ERISA) guidelines and is exempt from the testing requirements. Nonqualified plans include deferred compensation, executive bonuses, and split-dollar life insurance plans.

Notary is a person authorized to perform certain legal formalities, especially to draw up or certify contracts, deeds, and other documents for use in defined jurisdictions. Source: health.unl.edu

Notary Public: read the definition of Notary.

Note Payable is a general ledger liability account in which a company records the face amounts of its issued promissory notes. Source: courses.lumenlearning.com

Notes are a form of debt security that requires obligatory loan repayment at a predetermined interest rate within a defined period. The notes typically have an earlier maturity date than other debt securities, such as bonds. Source: uslegalforms.com

Ombudsman is an official appointed to investigate individuals' complaints against maladministration, especially that of public authorities.

Option is a contract that conveys to its owner, the holder, the right, but not the obligation, to buy or sell an underlying asset or instrument at a specified strike price on or before a specified date. Source: lightspeed.com

Partnership is an arrangement between two or more people to oversee business operations and share profits and losses. Source: Investopedia.com

Pension Plan: read the definition of a Defined Benefit Plan.

Perjury is the offense of willfully stating an untruth in court after taking an oath or affirmation.

Personal Property is Tangible or Intangible Property that is not Real Property.

Petition is the title of a legal pleading that initiates a legal case, usually in a civil lawsuit, and seeks non-monetary or "equitable" relief.

Petitioner is a person who petitions a governmental institution for a legal remedy or redress of grievances.

Plaintiff is a person who brings a case against another (Defendant) in a court of law.

Power of Attorney (POA) is a legal document between the Agent and the Principal that enables the Agent to act on behalf of the Principal.

Principal is a person who establishes a Power of Attorney; the Principal names an Agent and bestows that person the ability to perform actions on the Principal's behalf.

Probate Court is a segment of the judicial system that primarily handles such matters as wills, estates, conservatorships, and guardianships, as well as the commitment of a person with psychiatric disabilities to institutions designed to help them. Source: wcalabama.com

Profit Sharing is an employer-based program with an incentivized compensation plan that gives employees a certain percentage of a company's profits.

Promissory Notes is a debt instrument that contains a written promise by one party (the note's issuer or maker) to pay another party (the note's payee) a defined sum of money, either on demand or at a specified future date. Source: sec.gov

Proprietorship is an enterprise owned and run by one person without legal distinction between the owner and the business entity. Source: Wikipedia.org

Protector is a fiduciary position commonly found in trust law whose job is to direct or restrain the trustee concerning the trust administration and its assets. Concerning Power of Attorney (Durable & Complex), the Protector's job is to safeguard the best interest/wishes of the Principal (primarily in a passive capacity) and provide basic administrative support (ensuring transparency) to the Agent. However, if the Agent violates their role as a Fiduciary, it is the role of the Protector to step in, relieve the Agent, and protect the Principal's rights and interests.

Put is an option contract that gives the holder (buyer) the right, but not the obligation, to sell an asset at a specified price (Strike) by (or at) a specified date (the expiry or maturity) to the writer (Seller) of the Put. Source: Wikipedia.org

Put Options: read the definition of Put.

Purposely: read the definition of Intentionally.

Qualified Retirement Plan is an employer-based program that meets specific IRS Code requirements in form and operation to provide retirement income to designated employees and their beneficiaries. Examples of qualified retirement plans include 401(k) plans, 403(b) plans, profit-sharing plans, and Keogh (HR-10) plans.

Real Estate refers to the physical land, structures, and resources. Real estate examples include, but are not limited to, the following: (**01**) Natural Property: Forest, Range, Wetlands, and Vacant Lot. (**02**) Residential Property: Primary Residence, Second Home, Vacation House, Duplex, Lot and Mobile Home, Cooperative Apartment, Condominium, Co-op, and Time-Share Unit. (**03**) Income Producing Property: Residential, Farm, Agricultural Land, Subdivision, Campground, Commercial (retail, office, and warehouse), Industrial, Hotel, Motel, and Marina Dock Space. Source: coursehero.com

Real Property includes the physical property of the real estate, but it expands its definition to include a bundle of ownership and usage rights. Source: Investopedia.com

Recklessly is a state of mind that indicates that the person fails to perceive a substantial and unjustifiable risk that the result will occur or that the circumstance exists. The risk must be of such nature and degree that failure to perceive it constitutes a gross deviation from the standard of care that a reasonable person would observe. Gross Negligence is comparable to Recklessly when it comes to legal definitions. Source: Ky. Rev. Stat. § 501.020

Short Put: read the definition of Naked Put Options.

Glossary

Simple POA is an Author's term for a Power of Attorney designed for short-term (less than five years) use with an Agent whose honor is beyond reproach and doubt.

Social Security is a social welfare and insurance program in the United States of America funded through payroll taxes, which provides individuals with retirement or disability income.

Special POA is an Author's term for a Power of Attorney designed for short-term (less than five years) use with an Agent whose honor is beyond reproach and doubt. The primary key difference that separates a Special POA from a Simple POA is that a Special POA has a limited scope and purpose.

Springing Powers is additional legal language in a Power of Attorney that delays the Agent's ability to act on behalf of the Principal until an event occurs, thus "springing" into action. Source: cloudways.com

Sprinkling Powers is additional legal language that gives discretionary decision-making powers to the Fiduciary, usually associated with the distribution of income or property.

Stock is a financial security representing the ownership of a fraction of a corporation.

Stock Bonus is an issue of Stock shares by a company in place of cash or dividends.

Stock Certificates are physical pieces of paper representing a shareholder's ownership in a company.

Stock Index measures a stock market or a subset of the stock market that helps investors compare current stock price levels with past prices to calculate market performance. Source: Wikipedia.org

Stock Market Index: read the definition of the Stock Index.

Stock Option is a right (not the obligation) that allows an investor to buy or sell a stock at an agreed-upon price and date. Source: Investopedia.com

Subservient Agent is an Author's term for a subordinate Agent or Delegate. Furthermore, a subordinate Agent shall refer to an Agent or Surrogate in a different legal document (Power of Attorney or Advance Directive) over which the Protector has authoritative power.

Surety is a person who takes responsibility for another person's performance or undertaking; examples include but are not limited to, appearing in Court or paying a debt.

Surrogate is a person that can only make Medical or Mental Health Care decisions on another person's behalf, especially when that person is incapacitated or incompetent. Rarely is a Surrogate court-appointed; however, it can be. Surrogate priority usually occurs due to relationship status, for example, Spouse ➔ Adult Children ➔ Parents ➔ Adult Siblings ➔ Adult Grandchildren ➔ Close friends.

Tangible Property is a physical property that is movable and not Real Property. Tangible Property examples include, but are not limited to, the following: (**01**) Tangible Person Property: Animals; Antiques; Appliances; Art; Bicycles; Books; Clothing, Fur; Cameras, Photographic, and Video Equipment; Computer Equipment; China, Crystal, Silver Bullion; Gold Bullion; Coins, Stamps; Collectibles (records, dolls, Sports cards, et cetera.); Electronic Equipment; Family Heirlooms; Household Furnishings; Furniture; Hobbies; Jewelry; Letters, Documents, Papers; Medals, Awards, Trophies; Musical Instrument; Pets; Photographs; Precious Metals; Religious Items, Artifacts; Sentimental Items; Sports Equipment; Tools; Wedding and Engagement Rings, and Watches. (**02**) Title Tangible Personal Property: Vehicles, Boats, Yachts, Aircraft, Airplanes, Automobiles, Boats, Motorcycles, and Motor Home/RVs.

Tax Credit is an item that reduces the income tax a person may owe dollar-for-dollar. Tax Credits are more valuable than Tax Deductions of the same amount.

Tax Deduction is an item a person can subtract from their taxable income to lower the taxes owed.

Tax Exemption is an item that excludes certain income, revenue, or even taxpayers from taxation.

Tenancy in Common is a designation of property ownership in a shared tenancy in which each holder has a distinct, separately transferable interest.

Tenancy by the Entirety is a designation status of ownership in property owned in a shared tenancy reserved for married couples to hold an equal interest in a property and survivorship rights, with each spouse owning 100% of the property.

Testament is an act by which a person determines the disposition of their property after death.

Testamentary Trust is a type of Trust that is irrevocable by design; the creation and funding occur after the death of its creator from the deceased's estate according to the terms of their WILL. The only way to change a testamentary trust (or cancel it) is to alter the will of the Trust's creator before they die. Source: Investopedia.com, smartasset.com, and independenttrust.com

Glossary

Testator is a person who has died and left a WILL or testament in force.

Traditional IRA is an IRA where the initial contributions are tax-deferred; however, the growth (capital gains, interest, and dividends) is taxable.

Trust is a fiduciary legal relationship in which the holder (Grantor) of a right or property gives it to another person or entity (Trustee), usually to reduce liability exposure and to safe-keep said right or property for another person (Beneficiary) to use and enjoy.

Trust Company is a legal entity that acts as a fiduciary, agent, or trustee on behalf of a person or business for a trust. A trust company typically deals with the administration, management, and eventual transfer of assets to beneficiaries. Source: Investopedia.com

Trustee is an individual (person or firm) that holds and administers property or assets for the benefit of a third party, usually serving in a fiduciary capacity. Source: Investopedia.com

Trust Maker: read the definition of Grantor.

Trustor: read the definition of Grantor.

Undue Influence is influencing a person to induce an act that would not occur otherwise based on their own free will or without adequate attention to the consequences. Source: coursehero.com

Uncovered Put: read the definition of Naked Put Options.

Wantonly is a state of mind that indicates that the person is aware of and consciously disregards a substantial and unjustifiable risk that the result will occur or that the circumstance exists. The risk must be of such nature and degree that disregard constitutes a gross deviation from the standard of conduct that a reasonable person would observe. Source: Ky. Rev. Stat. § 501.020

Warrants give the holder the right, but not the obligation, to purchase a company's stock at a specific price and date directly from the company. Source: corporatefinanceinstitute.com and Investopedia.com

Welfare Benefit Plan: read the definition of Employee Benefit Plan.

Will is a legal document in which the Testator writes out their wishes regarding the care of the minor child(ren) and the distribution of the assets after the Testator died to a Beneficiary.

Willfully: read the definition of Intentionally.

Withdrawal Receipts are written instruments acknowledging receipt of funds from an account maintained with the Insured by a depositor; examples include withdrawal slips.

Witness is an adult who is not a party to the transaction and thus is not biased. A witness ensures that all parties signed the legal document(s) and that no forgery occurred.

This page is intentionally left blank

Image Source

Firewood Seller – 1746 [1 & 2]

Wood Seller – 1872 [4]

Picture Seller – 1738 [1, 2 & 3]

Cooper – 1742 [1 & 2]

Flower Vendor – 1738 [1 & 2]

Walnut Seller – 1738 [1 & 2]

Edmé Bouchardon [1]

Anne Claude Philippe [2]

Etienne Fessard [3]

William L. Sheppard [4]

Black & White

Wood Engraving

Wikimedia Commons

Image Source

Photo

"Accounting"

Zadorozhnyi Viktor

July 28, 2013

Photo ID: 142368100

Standard License through Shutterstock

Purchase: Dec 23, 2017
Order ID: SSTK-06A07-B624

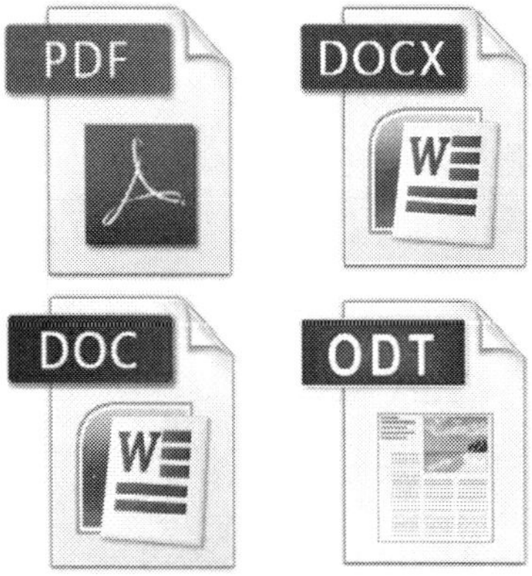

Graphic Art

(DOC, PDF, DOCX)

Jordan M. Groll

2008

(ODT)

Paul M. Paquette

2018

Use with Permission Jgroll.com

Graphic Art

Star of Life
Blue Version

Rod of Asclepius,
with Snake around it

Philippe Verdy

2006

Wikimedia Commons

Graphic Art

Paquette Publications

Logo by

Paul M. Paquette

2018

Image Source

Engraved Illustration

Matthaeus
Merian

Before 1650

"Ezekiel's Vision"

from Iconum
Biblicarum

Wikimedia
Commons

Types of POA

- **Simple POA** is for short-term (less than five years) use with an Agent whose honor is beyond reproach and doubt. The Simple POA has only one additional (**01**) option/safety feature: **Durability Provision**, hence the name "**Simple**." If Durability Provisions are active, this POA will also qualify as a "**Durable POA**."

    - **Key Details:** Names only one Agent, Effective Immediately, Define Expiration Date, and Built-In Safety Features
    - **Option:** Durability Provisions

- **Complex POA** is for long-term (greater than five years) use, preferably with multiple Agents to reflect the changing realities of life. These multiple options/safety features, if implemented, will create an administrative burden by establishing checks and balances on the Agent's power, hence the name "**Complex**." If Durability Provisions are active, this POA will also qualify as a "**Durable POA**." If Springing Power(s) are active, this POA will also qualify as a "**Springing POA**."

    - **Key Details:** Names Multiple Agent with successor's Agent, Variable Effective Date, Variable Expiration Date, Built-In Safety Features, and Sprinkling Powers
    - **Options:** Durability Provisions, Springing Powers, Agent Co-Power Sharing, Protector Provision, Delegate Provision, and Security Footer Settings.

- **Durable POA** is, in essence, a Complex POA, but with one key difference: the Durability Provisions are already active; thus, the durability provision is a "Key Detail" instead of an "Option." By default, the Durable POA will never have a simpler version due to the nature of the subject matter. This POA qualifies as a "**Durable POA**." If Springing Power(s) are active, this POA will also qualify as a "**Springing POA**."

- **Special POA** is, in essence, a Simple POA, best used sparsely with a limited scope and purpose. By default, the Special POA will never have a more complex version due to the nature of the subject matter. If Durability Provisions are active, this POA will also qualify as a "**Durable POA**." This POA is also referenced as a "**Limited POA**."

Power of Attorney

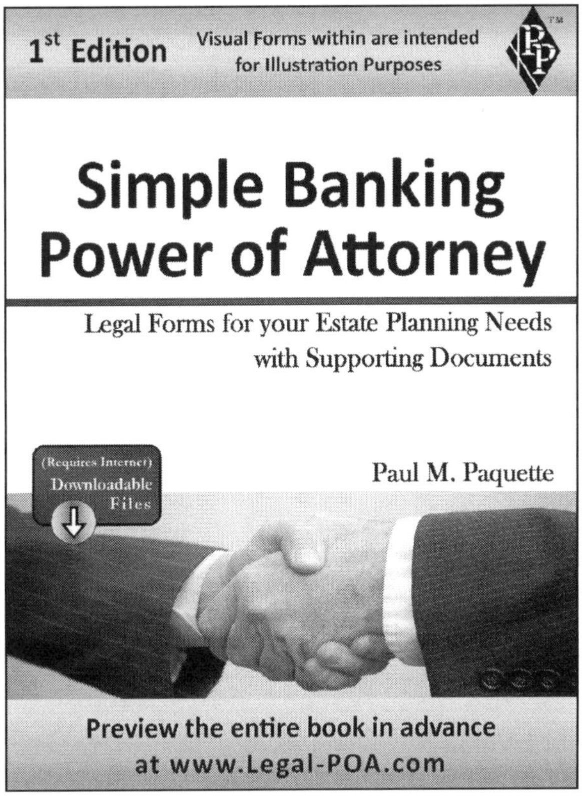

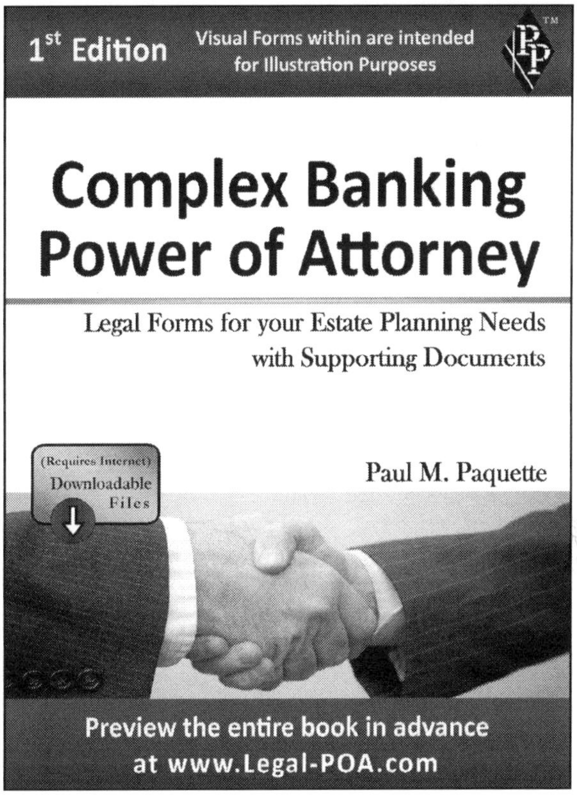

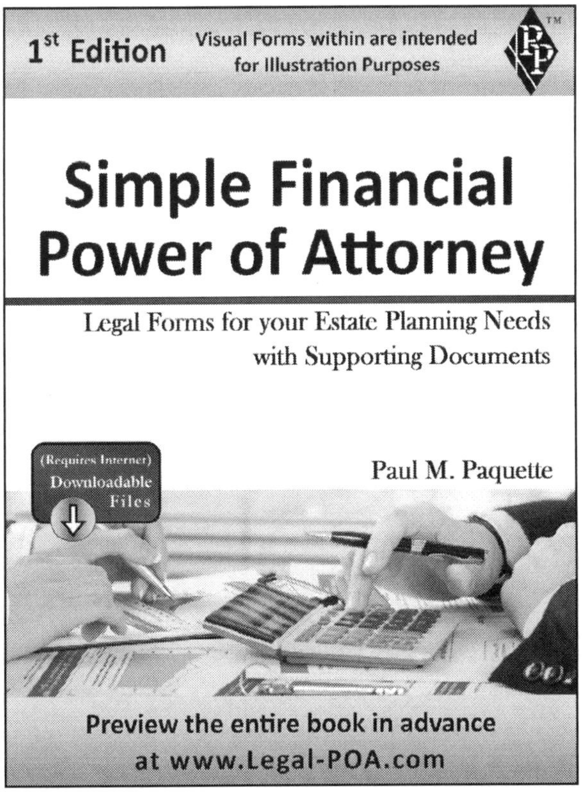

Power of Attorney

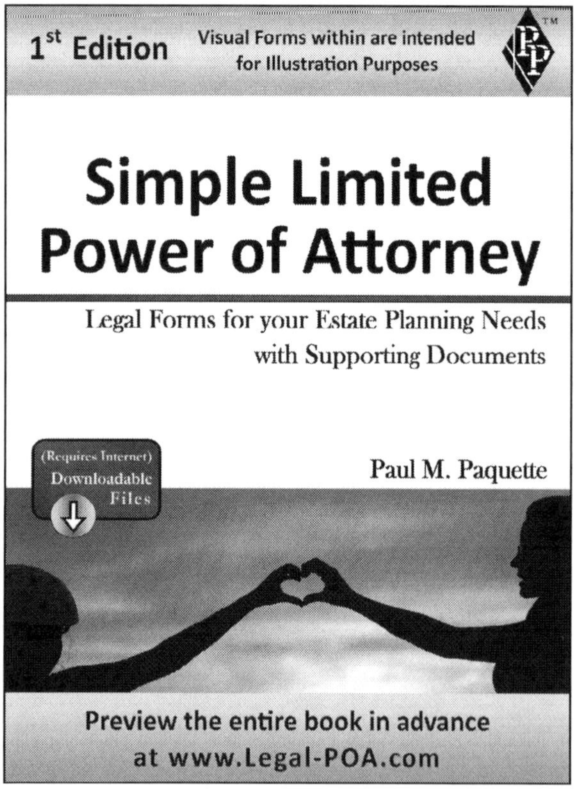

Power of Attorney

Power of Attorney

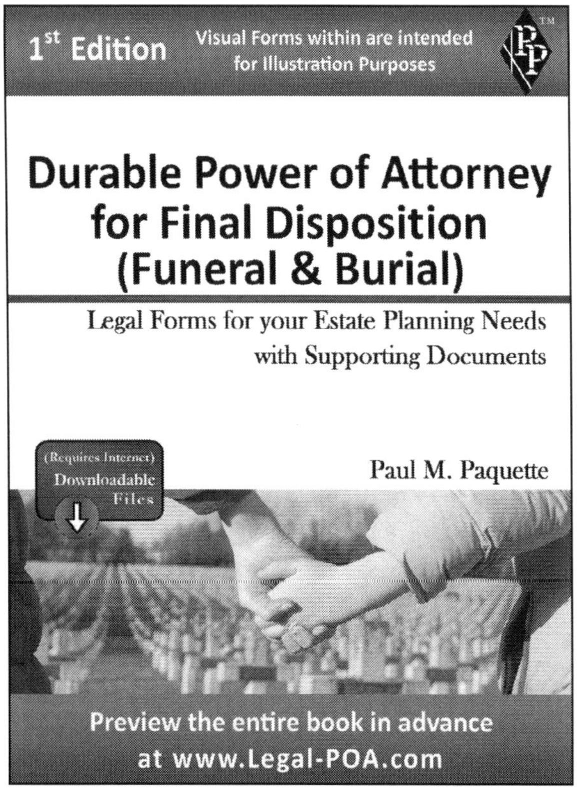

Power of Attorney

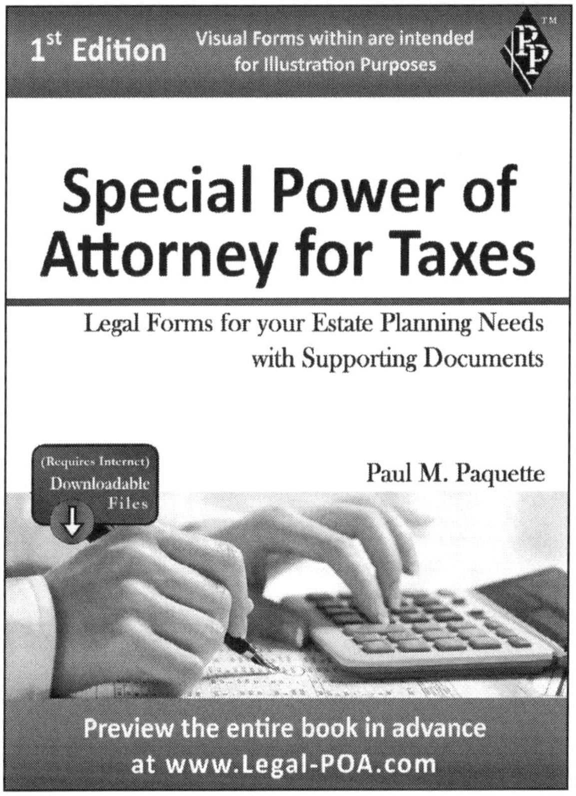

Declarations

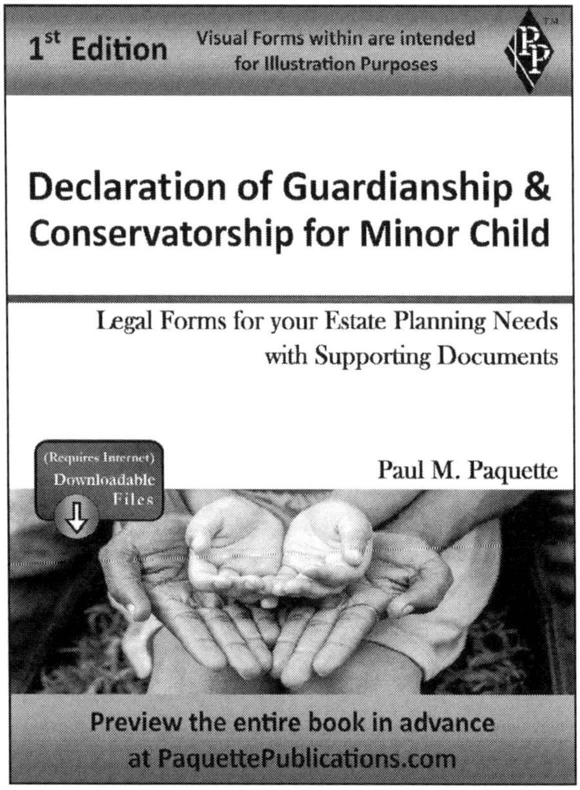

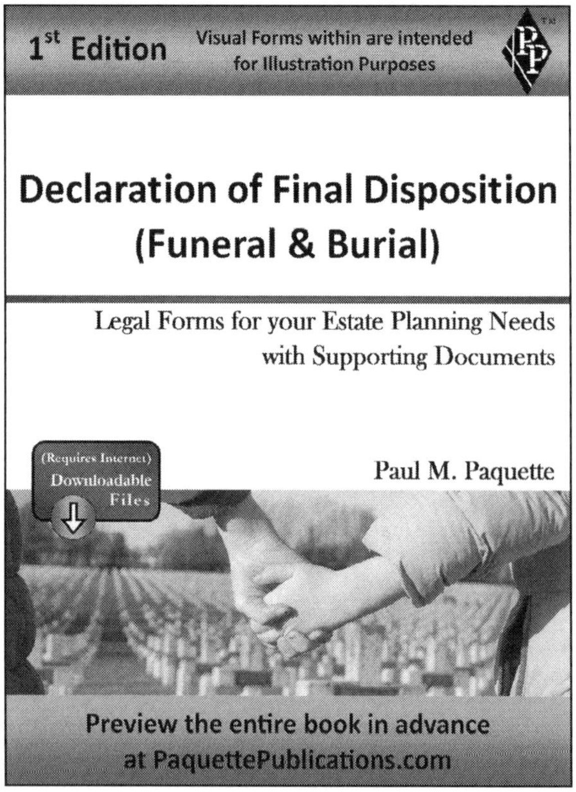

Declarations

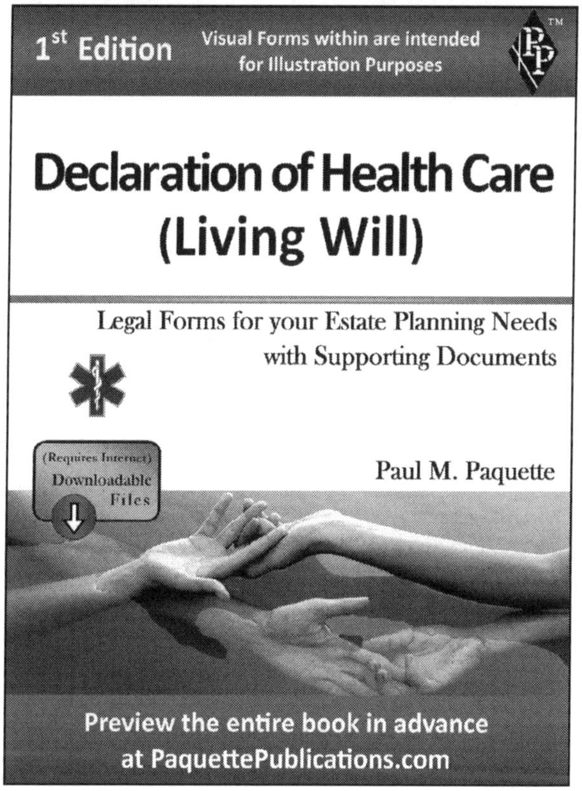

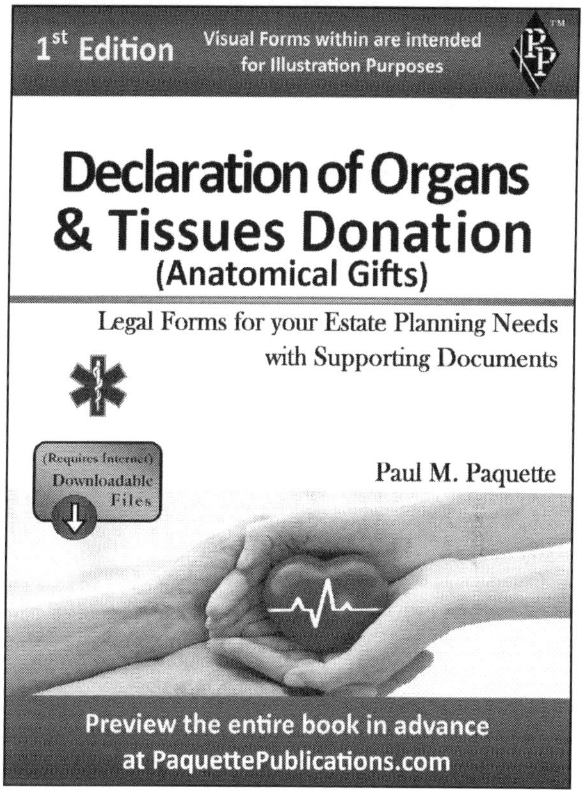

Advance Directives

Relationship Agreements

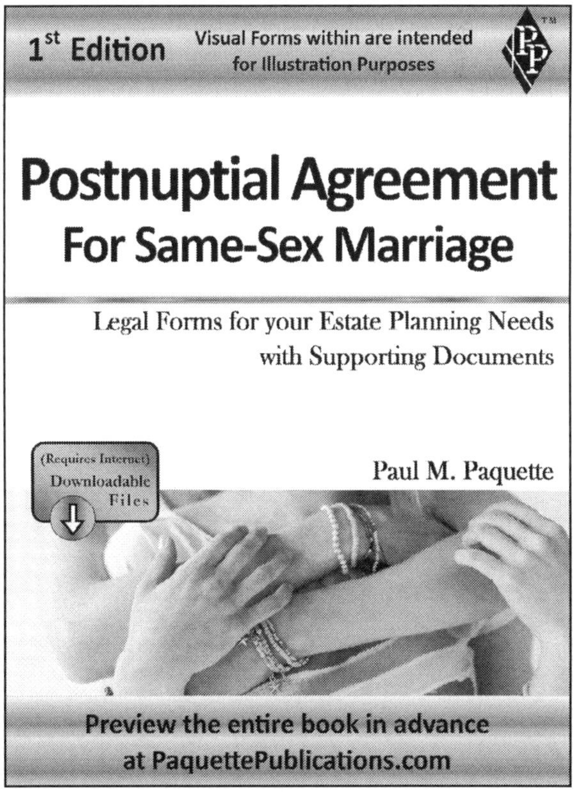

Relationship Agreements

Relationship Agreements

Word Processor Program

The Purchaser or User can open, edit, print, and save the Digital Files using a word processing program. Popular Word Processing Programs include Microsoft Word, WordPerfect, Open Office, and Libre Office. All word processing forms come in the following (**DOC**, **DOCX**, **ODT**). Paquette Publications does not offer the Word Processing Program or Technical Support for the Word Processor Program.

Portable Document Format (PDF) Editor

The Purchaser or User can open, edit, print, and save the Digital Files using a PDF Editor program. Popular PDF Editor include Adobe Acrobat Pro, Nitro Pro 11, PDF-Xchange Editor, Master PDF Editor, and CutePDF Writer. Paquette Publications does not offer the PDF Editor or Technical Support for the PDF Editor. Adobe Acrobat Reader is free to download at **www.adobe.com**. **Please Note:** due to encryption standards of **256-bit AES**, this PDF is only backward compatible (read/write) with **Adobe Acrobat X or later**.

Printer Setting

Depending on the printer's capabilities and settings, the Digital File (**DOC**, **DOCX**, **ODT**) may need editing to prevent cut-off text from occurring near the margins. The easiest way to solve this problem is to verify that the printer and margin settings are correct. If you still have issues, edit/fill out the Digital File, convert it, and save it as a **PDF** file. PDF files are easier, more versatile, and present fewer errors when printing. Paquette Publications does not offer Printing capabilities or Technical Support for Printers.

Modification Recommendation

If the Purchaser or User plans to make changes to the Digital File in question, it is highly advantageous that the Purchaser or User utilize the (**DOC**, **DOCX**, or **ODT**) file format. If the Purchaser or User is content with the choice selection, provisions, and options currently available with minor changes (if applicable), then it is highly recommended that the Purchaser or User utilize the **PDF** file format.

Downloadable Digital Files

Legal Disclaimer:

The Forms presented in this Book are available as a direct download from **www.paquettepublications.com**. In adherence with **Copyright Laws**, **Licensing Agreements**, and **Legal Disclaimers & Waivers**, these forms and their files are for personal and immediate family use only.

Legal Disclaimer required by the Distributor:

This Book does not have digital files (**PDF**, **DOCX**, **DOC**, and **ODT**) attached and does not contain fillable files or forms. As a courtesy, the Author has provided an Active URL Link to download the digital file (**PDF**, **DOCX**, **DOC**, **ODT**); however, the Purchaser or User will need to have an internet service connection, computer access, appropriate software, printing capabilities, and the ability and willingness to access the Author's website.

File Format Options:

The Digital Files are in the following formats: Microsoft Office Word (**DOC**, **DOCX**), Adobe Acrobat (**PDF**), and Open Office (**ODT**). The **PDF**, **DOCX**, **DOC**, and **ODT** are fillable and editable with the appropriate computer software.

Consent Checkbox:

To download these Digital Files (**PDF**, **DOCX**, **DOC**, and **ODT**), the Purchaser or User must first consent to the following Terms and Conditions (**Legal Disclaimer & Waivers**, **Licenses & Trademark**, and **All Rights Reserved**) which are present on the website.

Terms & Conditions

☐ **By checking this box, the Purchaser or User has read and agree to the following:** Legal Disclaimers & Waivers, License & Trademark, **and** All Rights Reserved **before downloading these file(s) (PDF, DOCX, DOC, ODT).**

submit

Download Links:

Using an internet browser (**Chrome**, **Edge**, **Explorer**, **Firefox**, and **Safari**), the Purchaser or User can download the Forms (**PDF**, **DOCX**, **DOC**, and **ODT**) presented within this Book from the following active URL Links:

Power of Attorney:

- https://paquettepublications.weebly.com/tc---cfpoa79---poa44.html

Supporting Documents:

- https://paquettepublications.weebly.com/tc---cd---support.html

Worksheets:

- https://paquettepublications.weebly.com/agrave-la-carte.html

Forms (Miscellaneous):

- https://paquettepublications.weebly.com/tc---all---forms---misc.html

Forms (Recommended):

- https://paquettepublications.weebly.com/tc---all---forms---recommended.html

Appendices & Glossary:

- https://paquettepublications.weebly.com/free---appendix.html

Extras:

- https://paquettepublications.weebly.com/free---extra.html

CD / DVD

This CD / DVD is designed (built and formatted) to work with Microsoft's Windows Operating System but should also work on Apple's Macintosh Operating System. **Please Note:** Paquette Publications does not provide technical support for computers or operating systems.

Print on Demand (POD) book
will have no CD / DVD available.

Please refer to the "**Downloadable Digital Files**" page to access the file(s) (PDF, DOCX, DOC, and ODT).

Please Return Disc with Book

Made in the USA
Monee, IL
05 November 2026

67845325R10118